LINUX ForYou
THE COMPLETE MAGAZINE ON OPEN SOURCE

Is Now Open
Source For You

A List Of Leading
Appliances V...

I0002671

Volume: 02 | Issue: 09| Pages: 112 | June 2014

OpenSource ForYou

THE COMPLETE MAGAZINE ON OPEN SOURCE

An *EFY* GROUP Publication

HOW FOSS POWERS UP
WINDOWS!

▶ **Getting Started
With Hadoop On
Windows**

▶ **Run Linux On
Windows**

▶ **Run WordPress-based
Sites On A Windows
Server**

▶ **Get Your DokuWiki
Running On Windows**

Be A Proficient
Web 2.0 Programmer

Bizosys Technologies
Uses **FOSS** As A
Gateway To Success

Manage Your IT
Infrastructure
Effectively With Zentyal

Contents

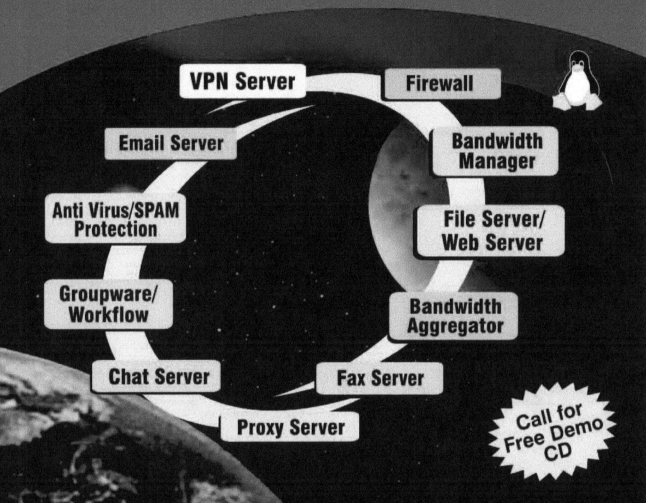

Contents

Editor
RAHUL CHOPRA

Editorial, Subscriptions & Advertising
DELHI (HQ)
D-87/1, Okhla Industrial Area, Phase I, New Delhi 110020
Phone: (011) 26810602, 26810603; Fax: 26817563
E-mail: info@efyindia.com

BENGALURU
Ms Jayashree
Ph: (080) 25260023; Fax: 25260394
E-mail: efyblr@efyindia.com

Customer Care
E-MAIL: support@efyindia.com

Back Issues
Kits 'n' Spares
New Delhi 110020
Phone: (011) 26371661-2
E-mail: info@kitsnspares.com
Website: www.kitsnspares.com

Advertising
CHENNAI
Saravana Anand
Mobile: 09916390422
E-mail: efychn@efyindia.com

HYDERABAD
Saravana Anand
Mobile: 09916390422
E-mail: efyhyd@efyindia.com

KOLKATA
Mobile: 08800094201
E-mail: efycal@efyindia.com

MUMBAI
Ms Flory D'Souza
Ph: (022) 24950047, 24928520; Fax: 24954278
E-mail: efymum@efyindia.com

PUNE
Manoj Chopra; Ph: 09223232006
E-mail: efypune@efyindia.com

GUJARAT
Sandeep Roy
E-mail: efyahd@efyindia.com
Ph: 09821267855

SINGAPORE
Ms Peggy Thay
Ph: +65-6836 2272; Fax: +65-6297 7302
E-mail: publicitas@efyindia.com

UNITED STATES
Ms Veronique Lamarque, E & Tech Media
Phone: +1 860 536 6677
E-mail: veroniquelamarque@gmail.com

CHINA
Ms Terry Qin, Power Pioneer Group Inc.
Shenzhen-518031
Ph: (86 755) 83729797; Fax: (86 21) 6455 2379
Mobile: (86) 13923802595, 18603055818
E-mail: powerpioneer@efyindia.com

TAIWAN
Leon Chen, J.K. Media
Taipei City
Ph: 886-2-87726780 ext.10; Fax: 886-2-87726787
E-mail: jkmedia@efyindia.com

Exclusive News-stand Distributor (India)
IBH BOOKS AND MAGAZINES DISTRIBUTORS LTD
Arch No, 30, below Mahalaxmi Bridge, Mahalaxmi, Mumbai - 400034
Tel: 022- 40497401, 40497402, 40497474, 40497479, Fax: 40497434
E-mail: info@ibhworld.com

SUBSCRIPTION RATES			
You Pay		**Overseas**	
Year	(₹)	(₹)	
Five	6000	3600	—
Three	3600	2520	—
One	1200	960	US$ 120

Kindly add ₹ 50/- for outside Delhi cheques.
Please send payments only in favour of **EFY Enterprises Pvt Ltd.**
Non-receipt of copies may be reported to support@efyindia.com—do mention your subscription number.

YOU SAID IT

 In praise of Ubuntu 14.04

I am a regular reader and a great fan of *Open Source For You*. The LTS version of the Ubuntu 14.04 release that you bundled with the May 2014 issue was amazing. I am sure that, just like me, a lot of your readers must have benefited from it.

Keep up the good work!

— *Anjjan Narayan;*
anjjan.narayan@yahoo.in

ED: Thanks a lot for letting us know that you like OSFY's content. It has been our constant endeavour to bundle the latest versions of distros and we aim to continue doing so in the days to come. Keep sending us your feedback as it helps us to do better.

 An article on Kali Linux?

I have been reading *OSFY* for the last two years and I must say that it is really informative and awesome! It would be great if you could provide some content on Kali Linux 1.0.6 in your magazine. I am sure a lot of readers will benefit from it.

—*Tanzeel Khan;*
khantanzeel@live.com

 Loved reading the 'SysAdmin Special' issue

 Sai Kiran Kuricheti: I have begun reading OSFY recently. The May edition (the 'SysAdmin Special') was very good and it really helped me a lot. Thanks for the same. Currently, I want to learn scripting like Bash and Python programming. I have tried out a few websites but couldn't understand them too well. Would you recommend something that would help me?

 Open Source For You: Thanks a lot for your words of appreciation. You can check our website www.opensourceforu.com for articles that you wish to read. If you do not find what you're looking for there, you can post this query on our FB page. The community will be able to help you in this matter.

ED: It makes us happy to receive such feedback from our readers. Your suggestion on incorporating content on Kali Linux is indeed a good idea. We will certainly consider it and let you know, once we include an article on the topic.

 Content on game development

I have been reading *OSFY* on a regular basis. I have a small request to make. It will be great if you published some articles on game design and development in Linux. I am a game enthusiast and an aspiring game developer. I see that thousands of games are now supporting Linux. Even Valves' new Steam OS is Linux-based. So do look into it.

—*Manas Mangaonkar;*
manas.man95@gmail.com

ED: Thanks for your suggestion and we will certainly try and publish articles on game development in the near future. We did publish an article titled 'Will a Career in Mobile Games Development be a Good Option?' in our April 2014 issue. If you wish to get a copy of the magazine, you can subscribe to http:// electronicsforu.com/electronicsforu/subscription/ subscr1.asp?catagory=india&magid=53. END

 Article on Red Language

 Kannan Ramamoorthy: I love reading OSFY. I hope your magazine will carry some nice articles on Red Language. How can one contribute to it?

 Open Source For You: Thanks a lot for the suggestion Kannan. We will definitely let you know if we come up with something on Red Language.

Please send your comments or suggestions to:

The Editor,
Open Source For You,
D-87/1, Okhla Industrial Area, Phase I,
New Delhi 110020, **Phone:** 011-26810601/02/03,
Fax: 011-26817563, **Email:** osfyedit@efyindia.com

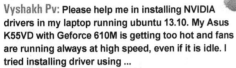
Vyshakh Pv: Please help me in installing NVIDIA drivers in my laptop running ubuntu 13.10. My Asus K55VD with Geforce 610M is getting too hot and fans are running always at high speed, even if it is idle. I tried installing driver using ...
- latest ".run" file from Nvidia website.
- command line.
- SoftwareCentre / Synaptic Package Mgr.
- I tried latest and some old versions also.
    In all the cases, I end up with ether a BLANK or BLACK screen after booting. Please give me some solution, Ubuntu is eating up my battery. If I could install the driver I can be a 100 percent Linux user.

Like . comment

Fahad Ahmed: I think this driver of the NVIDIA VGA is not supported on your laptop on Ubuntu. The problem with the CPU fan could be because of the voltage fluctuation, your computer might be getting excessive voltage..

Shadab Zakir Khan: You can check out this link. This might help. http://news.softpedia.com/.../How-to-Install-the-Latest...

Cindy Etheridge: Want a video editor (free) to use on my Samsung laptop. Can anyone please engligten me on the same?

Like . comment

Becky Lawson: Are you using Ubuntu? If yes, I recommend Kdenlive for this.

Yadhu Madhu: My 32 GB USB became RAW file format and now it shows only 30,6 MB. I am unable to format the same because it is showing write protected. Can you sugegst how should I fix it up?

Like . comment

Rahul Ghose: You can try gparted. This will definitely help.

Kripa Shankar: Have you tried "Ubuntu 14.04? Let me know your experience with the same.

Like . comment

Kevin C Nelson: I am using it right now and it runs smoothly. It updates for bugs and the bugs gave been quickly fixed so far. As of now, Ubuntu 14.04 works fine.

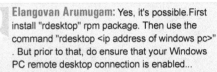
Jatin Bhardwaj: Is it possible to take the virtual connection (or remote desktop) of Windows from Red Hat Linux?

Like . comment

Elangovan Arumugam: Yes, it's possible.First install "rdesktop" rpm package. Then use the command "rdesktop <ip address of windows pc>" . But prior to that, do ensure that your Windows PC remote desktop connection is enabled...

Jatin Bhardwaj: Thanks a lot! I don't how to work with the USB drive in Red Hat. I have tried the same commands for CD/DVD mounting but to no benefits.

Elangovan Arumugam: What's the filesystem format of your USB drive? If it is NTFS, it means you can't. You need a third party software.

Jatin Bhardwaj: Which software sir? I think we have to format the USB in vfat to use in Red Hat first.

Elangovan Arumugam: Yes. Red Hat has the default access to vfat and fat.. But you can use NTFS also. You would be needing additional package, so that you can access the NTFS partition of Windows as well..

Jatin Bhardwaj: What kind of software is required?

Elangovan Arumugam: Package name is "fuse-ntfs-3g" in rpm.

Jatin Bhardwaj: Thanks! So it means that using this we can use the hard disk partition too?

Elangovan Arumugam: Yes. If you have dual boot with Windows and Linux, you can access Windows partition by working on Linux.

Varun Kharbanda: Can anyone please tell me some applications which can be used as cloud sync like Evernote, Dropbox for these platforms Windows, Linux, Android and Windows phone too. But I want enough space like 1 GB at least. Thank you so much in advance.

Like . comment

Utsav TecLuv Rana: Go for Google Drive,OneDrive or Box.

Friedrich Makkink: Have you tried Ubuntu One? I think this is a good option

 **LIFERAY.**

Give web visitors
what they're looking for

BUILD A SOLUTION THAT WILL DELIGHT YOUR AUDIENCE AND DELIVER LONG-TERM VALUE

Enterprise

Liferay is the premier open source portal for the enterprise and satisfies market demands for a light, flexible portal platform across multiple industries.

Open Source

In development since 2000, Liferay Portal has become the world's most popular open source portal platform. It has over 5 million total downloads and a community of over 100,000 users.

For Life

Liferay supports non-profits around the world because we realize that life is more than just about making great open source software. It's about building communities for long term impact.

Try it for yourself:

Liferay Portal 6.2 features over 70 tools for portal, content, and collaboration.
Download and install in just 20 minutes. https://www.liferay.com/products-liferay-portal/se-30-day-trial

Some of our customers...

🌐 www.liferay.com
f www.facebook.com/liferay
🐦 www.twitter.com/liferay

Liferay India Pvt. Ltd.
#19, 1st Floor, 1st Cross
P&T Colony, RT Nagar,
Bangalore -560032
Tel : +91 080 23544426 / 41532222
Email : sales-in@liferay.com

India's first Wi-Fi portable scanner from Portronics

Portronics has unveiled its new Scanny 6 Wi-Fi, the most recent to join the innumerable portable scanners that are armed with Wi-Fi. Scanny 6 Wi-Fi can be paired with any mobile phone, tablet or laptop with a Wi-Fi connection, using a browser or an Android / iOS app. It scans and then instantly sends the scans wirelessly to the Wi-Fi scan app on the computer, where one can organise, create searchable PDFs or send images to the cloud. It can also send scans directly (wirelessly) to iOS and Android devices with an included app.

The Scanny 6 Wi-Fi runs on rechargeable batteries and can perform scans anywhere without the requirement of a computer. It not only scans but stores the scans too, until it is synchronised via USB or Wi-Fi. Another great support feature of the Scanny 6 Wi-Fi is the display panel, which is provided on the scanner itself. Now, one can get that perfect scan, as you can see what you scan, allowing you to make amends if required. Jasmeet Sethi, a director at Portronics, shared, "We wanted to devise a power-packed scanner that might look small but is armed with a myriad of rich features. So, we introduced Scanny 6 Wi-Fi."

Price: ₹ 7,999

Address: Portronics Digital Pvt Ltd, 4E /14 Azad Bhavan, Jhandewalan, New Delhi 110055; **Ph:** 1800-1034241; **Email:** supportcenter@portronics.com; **Website:** http://www.portronics.com

Huawei expands its portfolio with the Honor 3C

In an attempt to make a bigger impact in the Indian market, Huawei has launched three smartphones, one of them being Honor 3C. Priced at Rs 14,999, the Honor 3C is a dual-SIM (GSM+GSM) device with dual standby and runs Android 4.2 (Jelly Bean) with the Emotion UI 2.0 on top. The smartphone features a 12.7 cm (5 inch) HD LTPS display and has a resolution of 720×1280 pixels. Armed with a 1.3 GHz quad-core MediaTek (MT6582) processor, the smartphone comes with 2 GB of RAM. The Honor 3C has 8 GB of inbuilt storage, which is further expandable via microSD card (the maximum storage capacity hasn't been specified). Packed with a 2300 mAh battery, the smartphone comes fitted with an 8 MP rear camera. Anand Narang, marketing director, Consumer Devices Business Group at Huawei India, said, "With these launches, we expect to make our base stronger in the Indian smartphone market that has been on a high since the last few years."

Price: ₹ 14,999

Address: Huawei India, 14th Floor, Tower C, Unitech Cyber Park, Sector-39, Gurgaon 122002, Haryana; **Ph:** 0124-4774700; **Email:** media.affairs@huawei.com; **Website:** http://www.huawei.com/en/

A classy mouse from Rapoo!

If you have a penchant for style, Rapoo's Compact Mouse M10 can be a great buy. It has a great design and runs on a reliable 2.4 GHz wireless connection for a smooth and interference-free mobile experience. In addition to that, Rapoo's latest energy-saving technology ensures uninterrupted use for up to nine months of battery life. The key features are:

- Wireless control over a distance of 10 m
- Works on a single AA alkaline battery
- Accurate cursor positioning
- 1000 DPI high precision tracking engine
- Six fashionable colours
- Nano USB wireless receiver

The Rapoo M10 comes with a choice of six trendy colours. It is designed to work in both home and office environments with the use of a reliable 2.4 GHz wireless connection. It works instantly once the USB receiver is plugged into the computer. The high precision 1000 DPI invisible tracking engine ensures responsive and smooth cursor control, letting you control your computer with ease.

Sunil Srivastava, country marketing manager at Rapoo India, said, "The Rapoo M10 is designed for the everyday user to work in a smooth manner. We are already getting rave reviews for our newly launched product."

Price: ₹ 899

Address: ELCO Systems Inc, 701 Brea Canyon Road, Suite 7, Walnut, California 91789; **Ph:** 855-777-2766; **Email:** rapoo.support@elcosystems.com; **Website:** www.rapoo.com

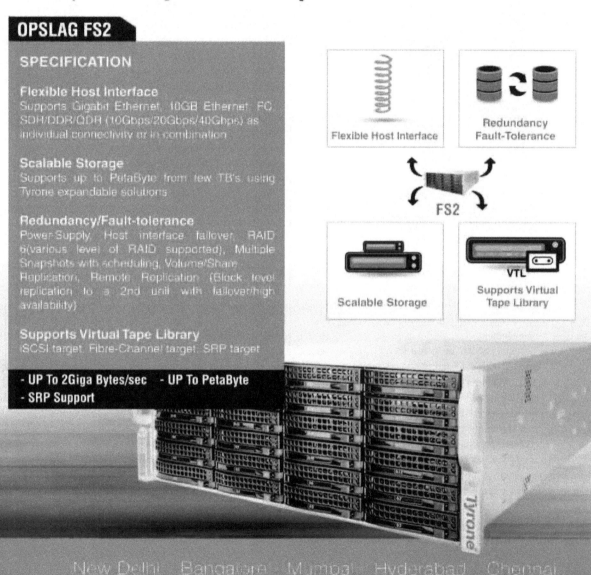

Trend Micro launches security solution for SMBs

Trend Micro has launched the Worry-Free Business Security version 9.0 to equip SMBs with enterprise-grade security capabilities that address and mitigate threats across endpoints, from desktops to mobiles. The offering is the only SMB solution available that provides complete user protection with integrated mobile device security, along with the option of cloud management.

"Since SMBs are more acutely affected by BYOD and consumerisation, Trend Micro is committed to providing dynamic, yet affordable, solutions that deliver greater functionality and ease-of-use. The ability to protect data across a business, regardless of who has access, is essential to a comprehensive approach to security. With integrated mobile device protection, Worry-Free Business Security 9.0 helps companies secure critical business information, whether in the office or while on-the-go," said Dhanya Thakkar, MD, India and SEA, Trend Micro.

Address: Trend Micro, 617, DLF Tower-B, Jasola District Centre, New Delhi 110025; **Ph:** 011 42699000; **Website:** www.trendmicro.co.in

A stylish tablet from Lava

Lava is on a launching spree. The smartphone vendor has come up with a 3G-capable voice-calling tablet, the IvoryS. Priced at Rs 8,499, the tablet runs Android 4.2.2 Jelly Bean, and features a 17.78 cm (7-inch) TFT LCD display with a 1024×600 pixel screen resolution. Armed with a 1.3 GHz dual-core MediaTek (MT8312) Cortex A7 processor, the tablet comes with 1 GB of RAM. The Lava IvoryS features a 3.2 MP rear camera and a 0.3 MP front-facing camera for video calling. The tablet is powered with a 2800 mAh battery.

Commenting on the launch of the IvoryS tablet, S N Rai, co-founder and director, Lava International, said, "The tablet is designed for young geeks who look for style and who want to own a chic device at an affordable price."

Price: ₹ 8,499

Address: Lava International Ltd, A-56, Sector 64, Noida 201301; **Ph:** 0-120-4637100; **E-mail:** care@lavainternational.in; **Website:** http://www.lavamobiles.com

Check out the new smartphone from Intex

Here is another addition to Intex's Aqua series. Intex has launched the Intex Aqua i5 HD, which is the successor to Intex Aqua i5. Priced at Rs 9,990, the smartphone runs on Android 4.2 Jelly Bean and features a 12.7 cm (5-inch) HD OGS display with a 720×1280 pixel screen resolution. The smartphone is powered by a quad-core 1.3 GHz MediaTek MT6582 processor. The Intex Aqua i5 HD sports a 13 MP rear camera and a 5 MP front camera. The smartphone comes with 4 GB of inbuilt storage, which can be expanded via microSD card (up to 32 GB). Intex is

also offering an additional 5 GB of storage space via its cloud storage service, Intex Cloud.

Price: ₹ 9,990

Address: Intex Technologies (India) Limited, D-18/2, Okhla Industrial Area, Phase II, New Delhi 110020; **Ph:** +91 11 41610224/25/26; **Email:** info@intextechnologies.com; **Website:** http://www.intextechnologies.com

OSFY Classifieds

Classifieds for Linux & Open Source IT Training Institutes

WESTERN REGION

Linux Lab (empowering linux mastery)
Courses Offered: Enterprise Linux & VMware

Address (HQ): 1104, D' Gold House,
Nr. Bharat Petrol Pump, Ghyaneshwer
Paduka Chowk. FC Road, Shivajinagar
Pune-411 005
Contact Person: Mr.Bhavesh M. Nayani
Contact No.: +020 60602277,
+91 8793342945
Email: info@linuxlab.org.in
Branch(es): coming soon
Website: www.linuxlab.org.in

Linux Training & Certification
Courses Offered: RHCSA,
RHCE, RHCVA, RHCSS,
NCLA, NCLP, Linux Basics,
Shell Scripting,
(Coming soon) MySQL

Address (HQ): 104B Instant Plaza,
Behind Nagrik Stores,
Near Ashok Cinema,
Thane Station West - 400601,
Maharashtra, India
Contact Person: Ms. Swati Farde
Contact No.: +91-22-25379116/
+91-9869502832
Email: mail@ltcert.com
Website: www.ltcert.com

NORTHERN REGION

GRRAS Linux Training and Development Center
Courses Offered: RHCE, RHCSS, RHCVA,
CCNA, PHP, Shell Scripting (online training
is also available)

Address (HQ): GRRAS Linux Training and
Development Center, 219, Himmat Nagar,
Behind Kiran Sweets, Gopalpura Turn,
Tonk Road, Jaipur, Rajasthan, India
Contact Person: Mr. Akhilesh Jain
Contact No.: +91-141-3136868 /
+91-9983340133, 9785598711, 9887789124
Email: info@grras.com
Branch(es): Nagpur, Pune
Website(s): www.grras.org, www.grras.com

SOUTHERN REGION

*astTECS Academy
Courses Offered: Basic Asterisk Course,
Advanced Asterisk Course, Free PBX
Course, Vici Dial Administration Course

Address (HQ): 1176, 12th B Main,
HAL 2nd Stage, Indiranagar,
Bangalore - 560008, India
Contact Person: Lt. Col. Shaju N. T.
Contact No.: +91-9611192237
Email: info@asterisk-training.com
Website: www.asttecs.com.
www.asterisk-training.com

Advantage Pro
Courses Offered: RHCSS, RHCVA,
RHCE, PHP, Perl, Python, Ruby, Ajax.
A prominent player in Open Source
Technology

Address (HQ): 1 & 2 , 4th Floor,
Jhaver Plaza, 1A Nungambakkam
High Road, Chennai - 600 034, India
Contact Person: Ms. Rema
Contact No.: +91-9840982185
Email: enquiry@vectratech.in
Website(s): www.vectratech.in

Duestor Technologies

Courses Offered: Solaris, AIX,
RHEL, HP UX, SAN Administration
(Netapp, EMC, HDS, HP),
Virtualisation(VMWare, Citrix, OVM),
Cloud Computing, Enterprise
Middleware.

Address (H.Q.): 2-88, 1st floor,
Sai Nagar Colony, Chaitanyapuri,
Hyderabad - 060
Contact Person: Mr. Amit
Contact Number(s): +91-9030450039,
+91-9030450397.
E-mail Id(s): info@duestor.com
Websit(es): www.duestor.com

IPSR Solutions Ltd.

Courses Offered: RHCE, RHCVA,
RHCSS, RHCDS, RHCA,
Produced Highest number of
Red Hat professionals
in the world

Address (HQ): Merchant's
Association Building, M.L. Road,
Kottayam - 686001,
Kerala, India
Contact Person: Benila Mendus
Contact No.: +91-9447294635
Email: training@ipsrsolutions.com
Branch(es): Kochi, Kozhikode,
Thrissur, Trivandrum
Website: www.ipsr.org

Linux Learning Centre
Courses Offered: Linux OS Admin
& Security Courses for Migration.
Courses for Developers, RHCE,
RHCVA, RHCSS, NCLP

Address (HQ): 635, 6th Main Road,
Hanumanthnagar,
Bangalore - 560 019, India
Contact Person: Mr. Ramesh Kumar
Contact No.: +91-80-22428538,
26780762, 65680048 /
+91-9845057731, 9449857731
Email: info@linuxlearningcentre.com
Branch(es): Bangalore
Website: www.linuxlearningcentre.com

Eastern Region

Academy of Engineering and Management (AEM)
Courses Offered: RHCE, RHCVA,
RHCSS,Clustering & Storage,
Advanced Linux, Shell
Scripting, CCNA, MCITP, A+, N+

Address (HQ): North Kolkata, 2/80
Dumdum Road, Near Dumdum
Metro Station, 1st & 2nd Floor,
Kolkata - 700074
Contact Person: Mr. Tuhin Sinha
Contact No.: +91-9830075018,
9830051236
Email: sinhatuhin1@gmail.com
Branch(es): North & South Kolkata
Website: www.aemk.org

Mozilla launches Firefox 29

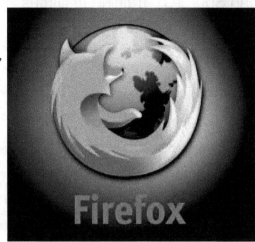

Mozilla has gone ahead and updated its popular Firefox Web browser for Windows, Mac OS, Linux and Android, bringing it to version 29 in its latest effort to offer a simplified interface to users. Firefox 29 is, according to Mozilla, "…the most customisable Firefox ever," boasting of an elegant new design and is currently available for download.

Firefox 29 brings along key changes to the menu pane and offers numerous customisation options. Users are now met with sleek new tabs and an overall modern look that places greater emphasis on the current tab while fading away other tabs in the background. The redesigned and customisable Firefox menu now features all the controls in one place, and lets users add or edit features, add-ons and tools. Users can now access the Firefox Add-ons Manager through the menu pane itself.

In addition, Firefox 29 comes with a new and improved Firefox Sync service that lets users access their 'Awesome Bar' browsing history, as well as their saved passwords and bookmarks across desktop and mobile platforms. "We reimagined and redesigned Firefox to reflect how you use the Web today and we are excited to introduce many features including an elegant and fun design, a new menu, customisation mode and an enhanced Firefox Sync service powered by Firefox Accounts," Mozilla's official blog announces.

Ubuntu 14.10 'Utopic Unicorn' to come out this October

All those who are still getting used to Ubuntu 14.04 Long Term Support (LTS) will need to hurry up. The folks at Canonical believe you should be pretty comfortable using Trusty Tahr by now, so founder Mark Shuttleworth has gone ahead and announced that Ubuntu's next iteration, the 14.10 'Utopic Unicorn' for servers and desktops, is set for release in October 2014.

"Now's a good time to stand united in favour of the useful over the uncolike and the utile over the uncous. Let's make something amazing. Something unified and upright, something about which we can be universally proud. And since we're getting that once-every-two-years chance to make fresh starts and dream unconstrained dreams about what the future should look like, we may as well go all out and give it a dreamlike name. Let's get going on the Utopic Unicorn," Shuttleworth was quoted as saying on his official blog.

Arduino will donate US$ 30,000 to promote the 'open' culture!

Arduino is always around to help out whether you're building a robot or a 3D printer! Based on the contributions of many other open source projects, Arduino is now gearing up to give back to the open source community, and will donate a whopping US$ 30,000 to promote the open source culture and innovation. Further, it has called upon the community to help select 10 projects that could benefit from this initiative.

"Arduino is based on the contributions of many other open source projects. Arduino is grateful to these efforts, and wants to support these and other initiatives through yearly donations. Each year, starting in 2013, Arduino donates to open source projects sharing the Arduino approach and philosophy," says Arduino on its official website.

Ubuntu 14.04 added to Intel's driver support list

Intel has reportedly added the Ubuntu 14.04 LTS version to the list of drivers supported by its GPU driver installer. According to reports, the new tool aims to simplify the installation and updation of drivers for Intel's graphics cards, allowing users to gain access to the best performance for their hardware and remain 'up-to-date with the latest Intel Graphics Stack for Linux.'

Ubuntu 14.04 LTS isn't the only version to be supported, though. Fedora 20 also has got support, while some older versions of Ubuntu are being deprecated or dropped from the supported drivers' list. Both 64-bit and 32-bit versions of the Ubuntu 14.04 LTS have received support for their drivers.

The bad news is for those using the older Ubuntu 13.10 Saucy Salamander OS. The support for the OS has been deprecated with this release. This means that users can still use Intel's tool to install the drivers, but no new graphics stacks will be offered.

Ubuntu for Android is no longer under development, says Canonical

Due to other priorities, Canonical has shuttered the active development of Ubuntu for Android (U4A). The news regarding the shut down of the U4A project first came to light when a public bug report mentioned the same. This was followed by an official statement by Canonical explicitly quoting that U4A is indeed no longer under development.

"We still believe that U4A is a great product concept and that consumers would welcome the feature. The development within Ubuntu for U4A is complete. To take the development further requires a launch partner in order to make the necessary modifications on the Android side. We are currently not in concrete discussions with launch partners, but we are still very much open to such a partnership," Canonical's statement to Android Authority said. Canonical is now whole-heartedly focusing on its own smartphone OS, Ubuntu for Phones, which is why U4A has perhaps been given the axe. "We are focused on Ubuntu for Phones at the moment. Therefore, we are not actively pushing for U4A. However, if a prospective partner steps forward, we are very much open to launching Ubuntu for Android," Canonical added.

Here comes the humble Pi-Phone!

The humble Raspberry Pi board never ceases to amaze us. Programmer-photographer David Hunt has now gone ahead and turned the Pi board into a US$ 160 cell phone. Besides, the developer has also expressed his desire to upload the source code for all to see and work with.

The working smartphone has the Raspberry Pi under the hood and is made of a bunch of off-the-shelf parts—an Adafruit PiTFT touchscreen, a SIM900 GSM/GPRS module and a 2,500 mAh battery. Hunt has also provided a video to demonstrate how the amazing device works.

In a related development, Raspberry Pi unveiled a new board that fits in the humble Pi's processor coupled with 4 GB of storage in the space of a tiny DDR2 memory stick. Pi's new compute module will allow circuit board developers to attach desirable interfaces into the small standard connector of the module. The compute module bids adieu to the tradition of using the built-in ports on a conventional Pi design. The module will come along with a starter IO board and is expected to be launched in June this year. There's still no word about the pricing, though folks at Raspberry Pi have revealed that large scale buyers like educators can buy the module in batches of 100 at a price of around US$ 30 per piece.

Torvalds honoured with a prestigious award

Linux founder, Linus Torvalds, has been awarded the prestigious 2014 IEEE Computer Society's 'Computer Pioneer Award' for spearheading the development of the famed Linux kernel using the humble open source approach. First established in 1981, the Computer Pioneer Award is presented to outstanding individuals whose main contribution to the concepts and development of the computer industry spans at least 15 years or more.

Torvalds has been the recipient of a number of highly prestigious awards—the EFF Pioneer Award, and the Lovelace Medal from the British Computer Society, among others. He is also an honourable inductee into the Internet Hall of Fame.

The world's largest social network for cricket, CricHQ, comes to India

The social network for cricket, CricHQ, was made available to Indian users on May 3, 2014. The Indian launch of the app was timed to coincide with the beginning of a programme called 'Meet Your Heroes', which gives Indian cricket fans a chance to meet cricketers from various countries. The programme is open to users who register on CricHQ to create their own profile.

In addition, CricHQ also has a partnership with Nokia (Microsoft), which has made the app available on the Nokia X and Lumia platforms. The 'Meet Your Heroes' programme, though, is available to all fans registering on the social network, either on their website, the mobile site or the app.

The CricHQ social network not only allows fans to create their profiles and enjoy cricket related features, but also hosts cricketers. This gives fans the unique opportunity to follow cricketers' lives by adding them on the network. According to Simon Baker, CEO, CricHQ, "Up until now, it (CricHQ) has mostly been for the administrators; but now with the social media stuff, there's more for the fans."

YouTube Mix now comes to Android

Global search engine giant Google has just made creating your YouTube playlists much easier. After hitting the desktop back in 2013, the YouTube Mix feature is now available for your Android smartphone and tablet. The feature auto-generates playlists of your favourite artists.

Thanks to this feature, all you have to do now is type in your favourite artist's name in the search bar and YouTube will auto-generate a playlist for you with the artist's most popular videos. On the downside, the results consist primarily of Vevo clips. Also, the feature might not work for lesser-known artists.

Google earlier introduced a VP9 codec system for enhancing safe 4k video streaming for YouTube. It teamed up with reputed electronic product manufacturers like Toshiba, Samsung and Sharp to make this system more user friendly. VP9 is not the first codec introduction by Google. The prior codec system, VP8, was also another codec-compressed form, which was introduced by Google under the BSD licence.

Picuntu 5.1 beta now brings Ubuntu 14.04 to MarsBoard RK3066 mini PC

Developers of the Picuntu Linux operating system have released Picuntu 5.1 beta (with the latest version of Ubuntu—v 14.04) exclusively designed to run on the US$ 60 MarsBoard RK3066 developer board. Picuntu is the customised version of Ubuntu Linux designed specifically for devices with Rockchip processors.

The developers have released the Picuntu 5.1 beta in three versions: a lightweight Xfce 4 desktop environment, a basic version and also a server edition with LAMP.

CALENDAR OF FORTHCOMING EVENTS

Name, Date and Venue	Description	Contact Details and Website
7th Edition Tech BFSI 2014 June 3-4, 2014; The Western Mumbai Garden City, Mumbai	This event is a platform where financial institutions and solution providers come together to find new business, generate leads and network with key industry players.	Kinjal Vora; Email: kinjal@kamikaze. co.in; Ph: 022 61381807; Website: www.techbfsi.com
Businessworld's BPO Summit June 5; Gurgaon	The event will provide a platform for thought leaders to discuss important issues which will shape the future of outsourcing.	Sakshi Gaur, Senior Executive, Events; Ph: 011 49395900; E-mail: sakshi@ businessworld.in
7th Edition Tech BFSI 2014 June 18, 2014; Sheraton, Bengaluru	This event is a platform where financial Institutions and solution providers come together to find new business, generate leads and network with key industry players.	Kinjal Vora; Email: kinjal@kamikaze. co.in; Ph: 022 61381807; Website: www.techbfsi.com
4th Annual Datacenter Dynamics Converged September 18, 2014; Bengaluru	The event aims to assist the community in the datacentre domain in exchanging ideas, accessing market knowledge and launching new initiatives.	Email: contactus@besummits.com ; Ph: 80-49637000; Website: http:// www.theglobalhighoncloudsummit. com/#!about-the-summit/c24fs
Open Source India, November 7-8, 2014; NIMHANS Center, Bengaluru	This is the premier Open Source conference in Asia that aims to nurture and promote the open source ecosystem in the sub-continent.	Omar Farooq-Product & Marketing Manager; Email: omar.farooq@ efyindia.com; Ph: 0995 888 1862
5th Annual Datacenter Dynamics Converged; December 9, 2014; Riyadh	The event aims to assist the community in the datacentre domain by exchanging ideas, accessing market knowledge and launching new initiatives.	contactus@besummits.com; Ph: 80 4963 7000; Website: http:// www.theglobalhighoncloudsummit. com/#!about-the-summit/c24fs

Github co-founder quits over harassment case!

Open source mainstay Github is currently in the news for all the wrong reasons. The company's co-founder and president, Tom Preston-Werner, has resigned after an independent investigation claimed that he and his wife had harassed an employee, a report claims.

According to the report, Werner's name wasn't mentioned until now, although most people had figured out which of Github's co-founders was being talked about. The employee concerned is Julie Ann Horvath, who was a developer at Github. She cited a hostile work environment as her reason for quitting.

The report says that Horvath claimed she had faced sexism and gender-based harassment at the company. She said that while Werner himself had been berating her in his office, his wife had been stalking her at work. This she said had continued for two years.

Horvath's outspokenness about issues related to women in technology is reportedly what concerned the couple. Horvath said they were afraid that she would undermine the company's image. The report also said that Chris Wanstrath, the company CEO, had been vague about the investigation.

Google ads will now link users within mobile apps

In order to bridge the gap between the traditional public Web pages and the increasing number of standalone, mobile apps popular with consumers, search engine giant Google will now allow marketers to run online ads within a mobile app itself. The move is directed towards extending Google's multi-billion dollar advertising business to the smartphones territory.

Google's ad revenue has been down in the dumps owing to the fact that more and more consumers access its online services on mobile devices, where advertising rates are far lower when compared to PCs. Google is finding it difficult to profit, even as mobile apps mushroom every now and then providing ample information to users—right from restaurant reviews to online games. Earlier, Google had begun to offer 'deep linking' capabilities with a limited number of participating mobile apps.

With this latest move, marketers can provide a direct pathway into their apps from the search ads. They can then display ads that they actually run on original Google sites. The new feature will initially appear only on smartphones running on Android and is expected to be available in the next few months.

OnePlus One with CyanogenMod 11s launched

Chinese smartphone startup, OnePlus, has finally launched its first smartphone. The OnePlus 'One' will be available at an introductory price of US$ 299 (unlocked, without contract) for the 16 GB model (roughly Rs 18,300). The 64 GB variant will be available at US$ 349 (roughly Rs 21,350). The One will come up with some real over-the-top specs. Let's have a look.

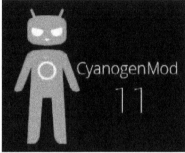

The OnePlus One will feature a 13.97-cm (5.5-inch) IPS LCD display with a 1080x1920 pixel resolution and Corning Gorilla Glass 3 protection. It will be powered by a 2.5 GHz quad-core Qualcomm Snapdragon 801 processor with an Adreno 330 GPU coupled with 3 GB of RAM. The device will run CyanogenMod 11S, a customised OS based on Android 4.4 KitKat. It will sport a 13 MP rear IMX214 sensor camera and a 5 MP front-facing camera. The device will not support any expandable storage. Connectivity options include 4G LTE, Wi-Fi 802.11 a/b/g/n/ac, Bluetooth 4.0 and NFC. It will have a 3100 mAh non-removable battery.

The OnePlus One will be initially available in Austria, Belgium, Canada, Denmark, Finland, France, Germany, Hong Kong, Italy, the Netherlands, Portugal, Spain, Sweden, Taiwan, the UK and the US.

Here's a Tor-powered Linux device that you can simply plug in to become snoop-proof!

Kay Anar and Gilad Shai, both long time TechCrunch Disrupt NY hackathon participants, have come up with a new device that you can just plug into the back of your computer to secure your connection from snooping. The duo recently demonstrated their hardware hack—the oRouter.

The oRouter is a Raspberry Pi-like computer that is powered by Linux and offers secure Wi-Fi access via the Tor network. The Tor-powered Linux device is an affordable alternative to actually downloading Tor. The oRouter is also an effective way to easily connect to the Tor network over mobile devices like Apple's iPhone, for instance. The demonstrated version supports up to 32 simultaneous connections. The oRouter consists of off-the-shelf components like a low-power single board computer, courtesy Texas Instruments, and low-power USB Wi-Fi dongles. Also, it requires just 5 V of power to operate.

Meet Cloudsto EVO, the inexpensive Linux Mini PC

Mini PC specialist Cloudsto is reportedly adding a new, small, low power Linux PC to its portfolio. Dubbed the Cloudsto EVO, this is a palm-sized computer, which will be powered by an ARM Cortex-A9 quad core processor and Ubuntu 12.10 software.

This is the first ARM mini PC that will have a VGA port instead of Ethernet. In addition, it will also provide support for typical PC display resolutions and an Ethernet jack, all designed so as to make the system a completely functional PC. According to reports, the Cloudsto EVO will be selling at US$ 160 in the United States.

Powered by a 1.6 GHz Rockchip RK3188 processor along with ARM Mali 400 graphics, the EVO has 1 GB of RAM and 8 GB of internal storage. It has micro-SD card support and Wi-Fi connectivity.

While this PC will be much slower than most other Linux-based variants, it uses much less power (only about 2-5 Watts) and is cheaper than others.

Linux Mint to be based solely on Ubuntu LTS

New releases of Linux-based distribution Linux Mint will reportedly be based on the Ubuntu LTS. According to reports, Clement Lefebvre, founder of Linux Mint, has announced that starting immediately, Linux Mint 17 (Qiana) will be based only on the LTS releases.

According to reports, this will reduce the complexity in going from version 17 to 17.1, 17.2 and so on. Also, fewer releases of the distro would mean that more effort would go into the development of the same package base over the next two years.

Clement also said that users will not need to sacrifice the latest updates of important applications, which will be backported to suit their needs.

What makes the hardware hack really interesting is the fact that you don't need additional software to make it run. You simply plug it in and connect to the available Wi-Fi network.

IBM unveils technology that tackles big data challenges with open server innovation model

IBM recently announced its new scale-out POWER-8 based Power Systems servers at the Open Innovation Summit in San Francisco. Built for an era of Big Data, the new scale-out IBM Power Systems servers are

the result of a US$ 2.4 billion investment, over three years of development and the ability to tap into hundreds of IBM patents—underscoring IBM's singular commitment to providing higher-value, open technologies to clients. Recognising Linux as a driving force for innovation, last year, IBM committed US$ 1 billion to new Linux and other open source technologies for IBM's Power Systems servers. Major investments included new products, a growing network of five Power Systems Linux Centres around the world and the Power Development Platform, a no-charge development cloud for developers to test and port x86-based applications to the Power platform.

IBM is offering the latest release of Ubuntu Server, Ubuntu OpenStack and Canonical's Juju cloud orchestration tools on the new Power Systems and all future POWER8-based systems. This complements the existing support from IBM for Red Hat and SUSE Linux operating system distributions on its complete line-up of Power Systems.

Ubuntu 12.10 will no longer be supported

Following 18 months of official support, Canonical has finally pulled the curtains down on Ubuntu 12.10 Quantal Quetzal. Ubuntu 12.10 is no longer supported, so users are advised to upgrade to Ubuntu 14.04 via Ubuntu 13.10.

Ubuntu 12.10 was released on October 18, 2012. Canonical founder, Mark Shuttleworth, had announced that Ubuntu 12.10 would be named Quantal Quetzal in

April 2012, and it was first in a series of three releases before the next LTS release. Meanwhile, support for the 13.10 release will also end this July. As such, Ubuntu's latest release, 14.04 LTS, is the only viable option for long term Ubuntu users.

Ubuntu's latest release for the desktop comes with a slew of performance improvements. Users will notice a slicker experience, with improvements to the Unity UI. The release also includes all the tools required for business usage, including the remote delivery of applications, compatibility with Windows file formats, browser-based cloud solutions and the Microsoft Office compatible Libre Office suite. You now get the option to use Unity 8, which is also the UI used on mobile versions of the OS—a major step forward in what Canonical terms 'complete convergence'. Further, the Ubuntu app store will come with a slew of converged apps that will give developers the freedom to write code once, yet make it usable on a string of devices and screen sizes.

HP to Invest Over $1 Billion in Open Source Cloud Products and Platforms

HP has demonstrated its commitment to open source technologies with the announcement of major investments in open source cloud products and platforms. The company recently announced HP Helion, a portfolio of cloud products and services. HP claims that its new offering will enable organisations to build, manage and consume workloads in hybrid IT environments.

With these offerings, HP is banking on OpenStack technology, an area in which it is a major investor and contributor. Ramachandran V, director, Sales–Cloud Division, said, "We are one of the leading players in the OpenStack consortium. Two of our people are amongst the board of directors for the consortium. So, one can imagine how serious we are about OpenStack technology and about 'openness'. "

HP Helion incorporates existing HP cloud offerings, new OpenStack technology–based products, and professional and support services under a unified portfolio to help meet customers' specific business requirements. The new HP Helion cloud products and services join the company's existing portfolio of hybrid cloud computing offerings, including the next-generation HP CloudSystem, which was recently ranked as the leader in the Forrester Wave report for Private Cloud Solutions(1). The new products include HP Cloud Services Automation (CSA) software for managing hybrid IT environments, HP's managed virtual private cloud offering and a range of cloud professional services.

The company plans to invest more than US$ 1 billion over the next two years on cloud-related products and engineering initiatives, professional services and on expanding HP Helion's global reach. With this announcement, HP has displayed its commitment to OpenStack technology and the delivery of hybrid IT solutions. Explaining this major investment in open source technologies and the cloud, Ramachandran said, "We will make this investment on a global level. HP has bet heavily on the cloud and we have proclaimed this at multiple forums. The cloud is clearly the most important place to be in and we believe that we have the best of solutions, services and transformations possible for enterprises. We have many customers running traditional IT. The road for them is to get on the cloud-enabled model. If we don't help those customers to transform, and get the outcomes that they are expecting, I don't think we would be doing justice to the kind of relationships that we have built over many years. So we had to be ready for our customers—for their end-to-end journey onto the cloud, and that is where we felt that we need to have our own products and technologies.

"For the past three years, we have been offering products in this space but the new addition to our portfolio that we are talking about is very unique. This is a cloud deployment tool that is downloadable in a USB drive and can be plugged into a machine.

It has got the desired pre-requisites and it can be set up with just a few clicks. This kind of ease was not possible before this product was launched. We have a complete stack ready for our customers."

HP has been running OpenStack cloud services at scale in enterprise environments for over three years. Ramachandran adds, "We understand that organisations require solutions that are open, secure and agile. As a founding platinum member of the OpenStack Foundation and a leader in the OpenStack and Cloud Foundry communities, HP has taken a central role in developing technologies that are built to meet enterprise requirements, and to deliver OpenStack technologies and Cloud Foundry-based solutions to the global marketplace."

The challenges for customers today are not restricted to just getting on the cloud. The challenges include how to manage, control and scale applications in a hybrid environment that spans multiple technology approaches. Aman Dokania, vice president and general manager, Cloud Division, HP Asia Pacific and Japan, states, "HP Helion provides the solutions and expertise customers need to select the right deployment model for their needs, in order to obtain the greatest return on their investment."

As part of the HP Helion portfolio, the company is introducing several new cloud products and services, including the following.

- *HP Helion OpenStack Community Edition:* This is a commercial product line of OpenStack that is delivered, tested and supported by HP. The community edition is available as a free version that is ideal for proofs of concept, pilots and basic production workloads. An enhanced commercial edition that addresses the needs of global enterprises and service providers will be released in the coming months.
- *HP Helion Development Platform:* A Platform as a Service (PaaS) based on Cloud Foundry, it offers IT departments and developers an open platform to build, deploy and manage applications quickly and easily. HP plans to release a preview version later this year.
- *HP's OpenStack Technology Indemnification Program:* This program protects qualified customers using HP Helion OpenStack code from third-party patent, copyright and trade-secret infringement claims directed to OpenStack code alone or in combination with Linux code.
- *HP Helion OpenStack Professional Services:* This is a new practice comprising HP's experienced team of consultants, engineers and cloud technologists to assist customers with cloud planning, implementation and operational needs. END

By: Diksha P Gupta

The author is senior assistant editor at EFY.

How to Select the Right
UTM Appliance for SMEs

With the rise of the cyber crooks in virtual space, a robust security solution has become a critical need for small and medium businesses. Unified Threat Management (UTM) appliances are meant to combat virtual intrusions and provide a security net to businesses.

The growing instances of complex, sophisticated virtual crimes can be a major threat to any business, irrespective of its size, and can impact its smooth functioning in a major way. Given that many small and medium enterprises have budgets for only a restricted number of IT staff members and limited security services, it's not surprising that the market for Unified Threat Management (UTM) appliances is growing steadily.

A UTM refers to a comprehensive security product that brings down virtual intrusion against numerous security threats. A UTM appliance is a single, cost-effective and easy-to-manage appliance that can be a better solution compared to various security software products running on separate servers. A UTM product typically includes a firewall, antivirus software, content filtering and a spam filter, all in a single cohesive package.

A UTM provides the following functionalities:
- Standard network firewall
- Remote access and site-to-site virtual private network (VPN) support
- Web security gateway functionality (anti-malware, as well as URL and content filtering)
- Network intrusion prevention focused on blocking attacks against PCs and servers

Besides the above, most UTMs provide other features like email security, Web application firewalls, and data loss prevention systems.

Key factors to be considered while buying a UTM appliance for your business

While looking for a robust UTM appliance in the market, the first thing you need to keep in mind is that it should fulfil and suit your specific requirements. That apart, factors like pricing and flexibility also play a key role when it comes to buying a suitable UTM product. It is important to establish whether you will have to pay for functionality such as email security even if you don't need it, or whether you can select only the security features you need.

Ease of deployment, configuration and management: An SME should ensure that its IT team is well-trained and has the requisite skillsets to effectively handle the UTM appliances. A simplified unified Web interface can make advanced security features accessible to relatively unskilled staff.

Ease and speed of adding additional services: While buying a UTM product, check if the UTM solution comes with extra security features without any additional costs like licensing fees. Else, you would have to regularly upgrade the UTM's software and firmware.

Resources of the vendor: An SME should also check how good the security research labs of the vendor are, and whether the R&D team will be able to provide new security features as updates to products already sold, as they become available elsewhere in the market. If that is not the case, the UTM will not meet your security needs in the long run.

Ability to deal with remote offices and mobile workers: Unless you plan on deploying UTMs at a number of locations, you'll need to link your branch offices to your UTM. Employees on the go will also have to connect to it via a VPN. It's therefore important to choose an appliance that can manage sufficient incoming connections, and one that offers a variety of VPN connections — possibly including support for Android tablet devices if employees use them.

Regulatory requirements: Another important factor that an SME must look for is whether the UTM provides the essential functionalities to let your enterprise pass a compliance audit.

According to Sunil Sharma, VP, Sales and Operations, India

and SAARC, Cyberoam, a security appliance that balances security with smooth business connectivity and productivity should be the one to look out for. "At Cyberoam, our solutions are prepared keeping this core philosophy in mind so as to ensure that security does not become a bottleneck at any point in time. Moreover, we offer multiple next-generation security features on appliances such as advanced application controls, a Web application firewall, online reporting and logging, advanced threat protection, VPN, multiple link management, etc. We also support 3G, 4G and WiMAX connectivity and are IPv6 ready. Our flexi port (XP) range of appliances empowers SMEs to expand their business without incurring larger security costs," shares Sharma.

Some of the UTM products available in the market

Cyberoam CR CR2500iNG

The CR2500iNG UTM appliance from Cyberoam offers a multitude of security and threat prevention features. The appliance has Layer 8 identity-based technology that offers enterprises actionable intelligence and controls. Cyberoam NGFW appliances offer application inspection and control, website filtering, HTTPS inspection, an intrusion prevention system, VPN (IPSec and SSL) and granular bandwidth controls. Additional security features like WAF (Web Application Firewall), a gateway anti-virus and anti-spam are also available.

"Cyberoam Next Generation Firewalls and UTMs offer comprehensive security to organisations, ranging from large enterprises to small branch offices. Multiple security features integrated over a single, Layer 8 identity-based platform make security simple, yet highly effective. Cyberoam's virtual network security appliances can be deployed as next-generation firewalls or UTMs, and offer industry-leading network security to virtual data centres and virtualised networks. Features include an on-appliance WAF, on appliance logging and reporting solutions, flexi-ports (XP), YouTube for Schools, 4-eye authentication, SMS authentication, and outbound spam protection to meet the security requirements of every organisation," says Sharma.

Sharma adds that the Cyberoam Global Support Management Centre (GSMC) is committed to ensuring the desired consistency, traceability and readiness to augment the customer experience with excellent technical support services that are ISO 2000:2011 certified. Cyberoam provides technical and product support, and customer care with its GSMC.

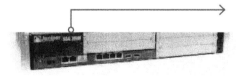

Juniper Networks SSG350M

The SSG350M from Juniper Networks is a high-performance security platform that helps businesses stop internal and external attacks, prevent unauthorised access and achieve regulatory compliance. It delivers 500 MBps of firewall performance and 225 MBps of IPsec VPN performance.

This appliance provides protection against worms, viruses, Trojans, spam and emerging malware delivered by proven UTM security features. Network protection features include security zones, virtual routers, and VLANs that allow administrators to divide the network into distinct secure domains, each with its unique security policy. Proven Juniper firewall security, with integrated routing and a variety of LAN/WAN interface options, provides SMEs with the ability to consolidate devices and reduce IT expenditure. The SSG series provides rapid deployment to quickly streamline widely distributed deployments while controlling operating expenses. Policy-based management allows centralised, end-to-end lifecycle management. The SSG series is easily managed through a graphical Web UI, CLI or NSM central management system.

Cisco SA500 series

Cisco SA500 series security appliances, part of the Cisco Small Business Series, are all-in-one UTM security solutions for small businesses. Combining a firewall, VPN, an optional IPS as well as email and content security capabilities, the Cisco SA500 series gives small businesses the confidence of knowing that they are protected. Base hardware appliances include Cisco SA520, Cisco SA520W with wireless features and Cisco SA540 with high performance. The features of Cisco SA520 include 200 MBps firewall throughput, 65 MBps IPsec VPN throughput, 15,000 connections, 50 IPsec VPN tunnels and two SSL VPN seats (upgradable to 25), and Gigabit Ethernet ports -- one WAN, four or eight LANs, and one optional DMZ/LAN/WAN.

According to the company, Cisco stands apart from the competition in the small business networking market as the only vendor that can provide a complete networking solution that includes switching, routing, unified communications, wireless and security—all of which can be configured and managed through a single interface.

WebRoam UTM Titanium-WR-1500

The WebRoam UTM Titanium-WR-1500 offers comprehensive enterprise-class security in a compact desktop form suitable for SOHOs and SMEs. It enjoys all the WebRoam security features as well as Intel's multi-core technology hardware facilities. WebRoam UTM Titanium-WR-1500 Multi-Layer security features provide optimised security and networking functionalities. Security, performance and price are taken care of for customers around the world. Systems administrators and mobile users can connect to the office network securely and with ease, from their laptops, smartphones and tablets. The WebRoam UTM Titanium-WR-1500 offers two solutions (OpenVPN and IPSec) for customers to connect their branches via a secure VPN. It offers central management with a wizard to facilitate complete configuration.

Dynamic Web-based administration and central management capabilities ensure quick, easy and secure administration from anywhere in the network. Automatic updates from WebRoam ensure that it is an active security solution that keeps your data, network and employees safe from the latest threats.

By Priyanka Sarkar

The author is a member of the editorial team. She loves to weave in and out the little nuances of life and scribble her thoughts and experiences in her personal blog.

Python Requests:
Interacting with the Web Made Easy

'Requests' is an Apache 2 HTTP library written in Python. Delve deeper into the topic and learn how it can be installed, and how Python Requests can be used to your advantage.

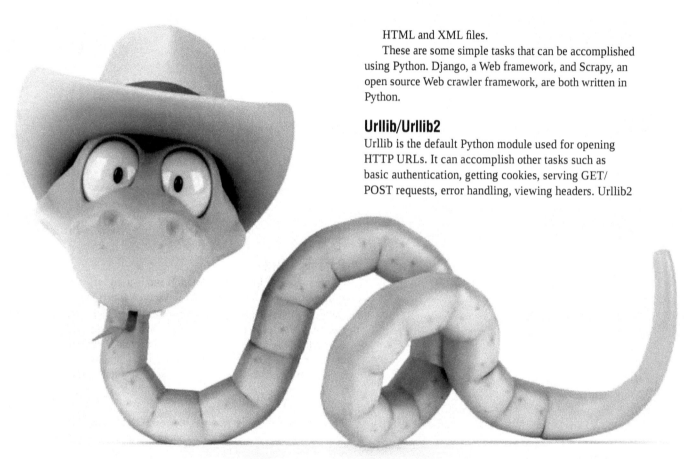

HTML and XML files.

These are some simple tasks that can be accomplished using Python. Django, a Web framework, and Scrapy, an open source Web crawler framework, are both written in Python.

Urllib/Urllib2

Urllib is the default Python module used for opening HTTP URLs. It can accomplish other tasks such as basic authentication, getting cookies, serving GET/POST requests, error handling, viewing headers. Urllib2

Python contains libraries that make it easy to interact with websites to perform tasks like logging into Gmail, viewing Web pages, filling forms, viewing and saving cookies—with nothing more than a few lines of code. Once a request is sent to a server, a Python script returns the information in almost the same way as a browser. Hence, the work done by a Python script is more or less similar to that of a Web browser. Some reasons why Python is preferred for accessing the Web are:

- Scripts can be written to automate interaction with a Web page.
- RSS feeds can be obtained and parsed.
- A Web spider to test your site or search other sites can be written.
- Beautifulsoup (a Python module) is used for parsing

is an improved Python module and provides additional functionalities to several methods. Hence some urllib methods have been replaced by urllib2 methods. One such method is *urllib.urlopen()* , which has been replaced by *urllib2.urlopen()* in the later versions of Python Requests. *urllib2.urlopen()* can accept an instance of a request class as an argument, which allows you to specify headers that are capable of fetching URLs using a variety of different protocols like HTTP or FTP; it can also accept a request object to set the headers for a URL request. On the other hand, *urllib.urlopen()* accepts only a URL.

In spite of having additional features, urllib cannot be completely replaced by urllib2 since the former provides important methods (e.g., *urlencode()*, used for generating GET query strings) that are absent in urllib2. Hence, methods from both urllib and urllib2 are accessed for accomplishing tasks. In spite of using both these modules, there are various drawbacks:

- First and foremost, it is unclear which module - urllib or urllib2 - is to be used and this is confusing, especially for beginners.
- In spite of urllib2 being an improved module, it does not provide all the functionalities.
- The documentation for both urllib and urllib2 is extremely difficult to understand and is heavily over-engineered.
- Even for a simple GET request, it is impossible to write a short script in Python using urllib2.

Here is a sample of the code required to perform a simple login:

```
import urllib
import urllib2
import re
import cookielib

jar = cookielib.FileCookieJar("cookie")
opener = urllib2.build_opener(urllib2.
HTTPCookieProcessor(jar))

url = 'http://example.com/login.php'
user_agent = 'Mozilla/4.0 (compatible; MSIE 5.5; Windows NT)'

data =
{
      "Submit": " ",
       "username":"x",
      "password":"x",
}

data = urllib.urlencode(data)
login_request = urllib2.Request(url, data)
login_reply = opener.open(login_request)
login_reply_data = login_reply.read()

login_success_msg = re.compile("Login Successful")

if login_success_msg.search(login_reply_data) is not None:
#Procede
else:
Print "Check whether you have given the right credentials"
```

Performing a simple login operation requires importing four different modules and writing large volumes of complex code. HTTP is simple and so should the scripts that access it be. Hence, it is vital to develop simpler and more efficient modules for accessing the Web when using Python.

Python Requests

'Requests' is a simple, easy-to-use HTTP library written in Python. The lead developer is Kenneth Reitz, who is also a member of the Python Software Foundation. The current version is 2.2.1, released on January 23, 2014, and it is compatible with Python versions 2.6.8 and above. Requests makes interacting with Web services seamless, and it overcomes most of the difficulties faced with urllib/urllib2.

Installation: Installing Python Requests is very simple and can be done using any of the two methods mentioned below:

- *Pip:* This works with Python versions 2.6, 2.7, 3.1, 3.2 and 3.3:

```
$ pip install requests
$ sudo apt-get install python-pip
             or
$ sudo apt-get install python-pip python-dev build-essential
```

- *Download from the source code:*

```
$sudo apt-get install build-essential libncursesw5-dev
libreadline5-dev libssl-dev libgdbm-dev libc6-dev libsqlite3-
dev tk-dev
$wget http://www.python.org/ftp/python/3.x/Python-3.x.tar.bz2
$tar -xjf Python-3.xtar.bz2 cd Python-3.x
$./configure --prefix=/opt/python3
$make
$sudo make install
```

Parsing JSON

JSON is JavaScript Object Notation and is used for transmitting data between client and server. It is often found that Web pages have JSON embedded in their code. Hence, while receiving requests, we often get a response in the JSON format, which needs to be decoded. Python Requests have a built-in JSON decoder, which helps in parsing JSON code. You can just import the JSON module in your code.

How to know if the response is in the JSON format: After making a get request there is a response object 'r' from which we can get information like the status code, header etc.

```
import requests

r = requests.get("http://www.example.com")
print r.status_code
print r.headers['content-type]

Output:
200
'application/json'
```

If the content-type in the header is of the type 'application/json' then the response is in the JSON format.

How to parse using the JSON built-in module and Requests:
- json.load(response) is used for decoding the response

- json.dump(request) is used for encoding the request

```
import json
import requests
response = requests.get(url=url, params=paras)
data = json.load(response)
```

Differences while decoding with JSON

The data we get after decoding JSON encoding data is different from the original data, as shown below:

```
data = [{ 'a':'A', 'b':(2, 4), 'c':3.0 }]
encoded_data = json.dumps(data)
decoded_data = json.loads(encoded_data)
print 'Original data: ' data
print 'Decoded data: ' decoded_data


Output:
Original data: [{'a': 'A', 'c': 3.0, 'b': (2, 4)}]
Decoded data: [{u'a': u'A', u'c': 3.0, u'b': [2, 4]}]
```

Features of Python Requests

- *Connection pooling:* There is a pool of connections, and a connection is released only once all its data has been read.
- *Sessions with cookie persistence:* You can make a session object and set certain parameters and cookie values. This allows you to persist these parameters and cookies across all requests made from the session instance.
- *Browser-style SSL verification:* We can verify the SSL certificates for HTTPS, as follows:

```
requests.get('https://example.com', verify=True)
```

For a wrong certificate, an SSL error is raised. If you don't want to verify the certificate, then:

```
requests.get('https://example.com', verify=False)
```

- *Proxies:* You can make use of proxies for sending individual requests:

```
proxy =
{
"http": "http://10.10.1.10:3128"
}
          requests.get("http://example.com", proxies=proxy)
```

- *Cookies:* We can get the cookies set by the server from the response object 'r':

```
url = 'http://example.com/cookie'
 r = requests.get(url)
 r.cookies['cookie_name']
```

We can also send cookies to the server, as follows:

```
url = 'http://example2.com/cookies'
cookies = dict(cookie1='This_is_a_cookie')
r = requests.get(url, cookies=cookies)
```

- *Response content:* Requests can automatically decode the response based on the header values. Using *r.encoding*, you can also change the encoding type:

```
r.encoding = 'utf-8'
```

- *Exceptions:* The various types of exceptions that are handled are:
  - Connection error: DNS failure, connection refused
  - HTTP error: Invalid HTTP response
  - Too many redirects: If the maximum number of redirects that is allowed is exceeded
- *Connection timeouts:* You can make the request stop waiting for a response after a certain time-interval. After this interval, the connection can close:

```
r = requests.get("http://example.com", timeout = 1)
```

Advantages of Python Requests

Here are the advantages of Python Requests over urllib/urllib2:
- Python Requests encodes the parameters automatically so you just pass them as simple arguments, unlike in

the case of urllib, where you need to use the method *urllib.encode()* to encode the parameters before passing them.

- Python Requests automatically decodes the response into Unicode.
- Python Requests automatically saves the contents, enabling you to access it multiple times, unlike the read-once file-like object returned by *urllib2.urlopen()*.
- Python Requests handles multi-part file uploads, as well as automatic form-encoding.
- In Python, *Requests .get()* is a method, *auth* is an optional parameter (since we may or may not require authentication).
- Python Requests supports the entire restful API, i.e., all its methods - PUT, GET, DELETE, POST.
- Python Requests has a built-in JSON decoder.
- Unlike the urllib/urllib2 module, there is no confusion caused by Requests, as there is only a single module that can do the entire task.
- Can write easier and shorter code.

A comparison of Python Requests and urllib/urllib2

Here are some simple examples using which you can easily make a comparison between Python Requests and urllib/urllib2.

Example 1: A simple HTTP GET request and authentication

Using urllib2: In this example, to make a simple HTTP GET request we need to call a lot of methods. Remembering the names of these methods can be difficult:

```
import urllib2

url = 'https://www.example.com'
username= 'user'
password = 'pass'

request = urllib2.Request(url)

password_manager = urllib2.HTTPPasswordMgrWithDefaultRealm()
password_manager.add_password(None, url, username, password)

auth_manager = urllib2.HTTPBasicAuthHandler(password_manager)
opener = urllib2.build_opener(auth_manager)

urllib2.install_opener(opener)

handler = urllib2.urlopen(request)

print handler.getcode()
print handler.headers.getheader('content-type')
```

Using Requests: The task of making a simple HTTP GET request can be accomplished in a single line when compared to the large code written using urllib2.

```
import requests

r = requests.get('https://www.example.com', auth=('user', 'pass'))

print r.status_code
print r.headers['content-type']
```

Example 2: Making a POST request

Using urllib2/urllib: Note that in this example we had to make use of both the urllib and urllib2 modules in order to write a script for a simple POST request:

```
import urllib
import urllib2

url = "http://www.example.com"
values = {"firstname":" abc ", "lastname":" xyz "}

header = {"User-Agent":"Mozilla/4.0 (compatible; MSIE 5.5;Windows NT)"}

values = urllib.urlencode(values)
request = urllib2.Request(url, values, header)

response = urllib2.urlopen(request)
html_content = response.read()
```

Using Requests: Here we do not require import multiple modules and a single requests module can accomplish the entire task:

```
import requests

values = {"""firstname":" abc ", "lastname":" xyz "}
r = requests.post('https://www.example.com, data=values)
```

Acknowledgments

I would like to thank Kenneth Reitz, lead developer of Python Requests, for designing and developing the Python Requests library. I would also like to thank my mentor and all the people who helped me to review this article.

References

[1] *http://docs.python-requests.org/en/latest/*
[2] *https://pypi.python.org/pypi/requests*

By: Sakshi Bansal

The author is a FOSS enthusiast and an active member of Amrita FOSS club. She has contributed to various open source projects such as Mozilla Thunderbird, Mediawiki. She blogs at *http://sakshiii.wordpress.com/*.

Embark on Your Programming Journey with AMP

Here is an insight into running Apache, MySQL and PHP (AMP) on Windows. The author leads readers through his own experience to point out where the pitfalls are. This article is particularly useful for newbies venturing into AMP.

The first time I tried to create a Web app was during my college days. It was to be an application that would act like a college management system. Since I was a newbie and the project was too ambitious, I discovered that I couldn't figure things out—the app never really worked. Of the many things I do remember was the fact that I couldn't set up LAMP on my OpenSUSE box. I was a power user of OpenSUSE, yet, after a couple of days, I simply couldn't get the LAMP stack working. I then decided to stop trying and begin again on a platform that I didn't particularly like to use for development —Windows.

Starting off

Linux is not always the best platform to start on, since most people are unfamiliar with it. Even power users can get confused and not be able to set up a development environment straight away. This is one instance where you ought to stick with Windows rather than go with Linux. As a beginner who has not forayed into Web development, on Windows you can at least understand the instructions and follow them, and almost everyone you meet has some understanding of it. The

ready-made packages for Windows require you to just install them to start working.

There are two ways to start off with the AMP (Apache, PHP, MySQL) stack on Windows: 1) Use a prebuilt package, and 2) Install the individual components and configure them to work with each other, manually. The first option is the easier one, which I would recommend. It is difficult to configure AMP manually on Linux as well as on Windows. This is largely due to the number of configuration files that need to be edited and the steps that have to be taken. Briefly, here are the steps you need to follow while configuring AMP manually on your system:

1. Install MySQL.
2. Configure MySQL parameters by editing the *my.cnf* file.
3. Install PHP.
4. Install the MySQL extension for PHP.
5. Edit the PHP configuration file (*php.ini*) to enable MySQL's support for PHP.
6. Install Apache.
7. Configure Apache to work with PHP.

There are chances of you getting stuck at many stages

in this process; hence, installing a preconfigured package is recommended for Windows. Preconfigured packages are software installers that do the steps listed above, for you. All you need to do is to install them and you are ready to go!

The one that is most widely used is XAMPP, which I recommend because it is popular—it means that if you encounter a problem, there will be enough help available on the Web. The second (and quite important) parameter is path names. Where you install software in Windows is an important factor, more so when you are running software originally built for UNIX-like platforms (or let's just say 'Linux' instead). Windows and Linux deal with file system paths in different ways, which can be annoying. The installation paths for the components (Apache, PHP and MySQL) are conducive to the Windows environment. The third reason for choosing XAMPP is that it comes with a simple service controller. So you can launch Apache and MySQL when you need them and shut them down when you don't. Fourth, XAMPP also comes with a nifty FTP client, which can be pretty useful when you need to upload your work to a server. The last reason is that XAMPP also comes with other necessary tools, which allow you to get started real fast; for example, the MySQL root password is set to blank, PhpMyAdmin (a Web or browser-based tool to manage MySQL databases) is already installed and there is a page showing 'phpinfo()'. Please note that the setup created by XAMPP is nowhere close to being secure enough for use on a production server.

Moving on with PHP on Windows

Installing PHP on Windows is only the beginning, to be followed by installing extensions, which is much simpler. Most of the necessary extensions are already installed. All you have to do is to enable them in the *php.ini* file and they will start working. So connecting to your databases or encrypting your data using PHP isn't a problem.

But as you move forward, it is important to keep in mind that PHP's primary target is not Windows. PHP is UNIX-world software that 'also' runs on Windows. One of the biggest problems for new programmers using PHP on Windows is the path names. If you open a file and you copy-paste the path from your Windows Explorer's address bar into your PHP script, it may not work—one of the most common problems.

File paths

On all UNIX-like systems, the directory separator is the '/' character. On Windows, it is '\'. At many points, this might cause some confusion upfront. While '\' might work at times when specifying the path in PHP, it should be avoided. The worst thing you can do with paths is to mix the directory separators in the same path, which will not work. PHP recommends that you use '/' as the directory separator on

Windows as well. So *C:\xampp\htdocs\project* should be written as *C:/xampp/htdocs/project.*

Line endings and IDEs

Development involves using other people's work—a library, a patch or maybe even a complete project. Linux uses the '\n' character for newline while Windows uses '\r\n'. This means that if you are using a piece of code which was originally written for Linux, it may not look pretty on Windows; at least, not natively. If you have been using a primitive text editor (such as Notepad) for coding, make sure that you get yourself an IDE or at least a decent text editor with more developer-friendly features. Notepad++ and Sublime Text are very developer-friendly text editors. Eclipse for PHP is a good free IDE while PHPStorm is by far the best IDE you can get for PHP, with many of its features currently not seen in most other IDEs. If you like Visual Studio, there is a plugin by Microsoft that allows you to write PHP with Visual Studio as well. Get yourself a decent IDE/text editor. These not only fix the viewing problems associated with line-endings but also come with some goodies that help you work much faster.

Servers

PHP is a scripting language for the Web. You do need a Web server to make it function and there are a number of them. On Windows, you have at least one extra option compared to other platforms – IIS. This stands for Internet Information Services and is the Web server developed by Microsoft itself. There are two things about it that need to be remembered:
1. It is switched off, by default.
2. If you are not going to work on C# or other .NET languages for Web development on Windows, it is better to use Apache rather than IIS. It does exactly what Apache does—serve Web pages. However, IIS supports Microsoft technologies, which Apache does not do too well. However, when it comes to PHP, the amount of help you get online with Apache is much more than what you get for IIS. The reason being that Apache works on Linux too, and with the exception of file paths, most solutions that work on Linux work on Windows as well.

And like I have already said, it is better to go for packaged AMP installations such as XAMPP which come with Apache. Enabling IIS would create a conflict with them.

Apache

Apache is the most famous Web server there is. What separates Apache from the rest is the amount of customisation that you can do. Having a threaded server or a non-threaded one, support for a very large number of languages as modules, handling multiple websites, managing permissions, customisable security levels are some of the most attractive functions that one can tweak the server to deliver. All of this means that there are chances that you can get one of those wrong and that would damage your installation. So first things first — if the server is working the way you want it to, try not to change it (unless of course you are trying to learn more about Apache Web server itself).

Do remember that for developmental purposes, it is better to keep the security a little loose, while on the production server, it must be as tight as possible. If you are able to run multiple Web projects using just 'localhost', so much the better. If you have two projects named 'college' and 'personal', it is better to run them from *http://localhost/college* and *http://localhost/personal* when possible.

However, this is not always feasible and we might want separate domain names to test things out. To create a VirtualHost in Apache is not a very easy task if one has not done it previously. To make a new VirtualHost in Apache, follow the steps mentioned below (which have been tested with Apache installed with XAMPP; the configuration file governing the VirtualHosts might be different for other installations):

1. Open *C:\xampp\apache\conf\extra\httpd-vhosts.conf* file in a text-editor.
2. Add the following lines of code to the end (explained later):

```
<VirtualHost *:80>
    ServerAdmin youremail@host.com
    DocumentRoot "C:/xampp/v-htdocs/drupal.example.com"
    ServerName drupal.example.com
    ErrorLog "logs/drupal.example.com-error.log"
  CustomLog "logs/ drupal.example.com-access.log" common
  </VirtualHost>
```

3. Save the file.
4. Open file: *C:\Windows\System32\drivers\etc\hosts* in Notepad and add this line at the end:
   a. *127.0.0.1 drupal.example.com*
5. Save the file and restart the Apache server.
   The lines you added in Step 2 play the following roles:
- <VirtualHost *:80>: This starts the definition of the virtual host and says that it should be reachable from all addresses on port 80.
- ServerAdmin: This is the email which is displayed in error messages and should be of the person who maintains the server.
- DocumentRoot: The path of the folder from where the files of this VirtualHost will be served.
- ServerName: The domain name to which this VirtualHost will respond.
- ErrorLog: This is the path of the file where the error log should be stored. It is relative to the Apache installation directory.
- CustomLog: Other error logs should be stored in the file indicated here.

- It is also important to make the changes in your hosts file later so that you can use the domain name of this virtual host on your machine.

MySQL

MySQL comes with XAMPP. If you are installing it outside of XAMPP, the wizard takes all the right steps. However, there are a few things to keep in mind:
1. The MySQL root password should not be forgotten.
2. The MySQL root password is set to blank by XAMPP, by default—this is not good for production servers.
3. You should try to have another user, even for developmental purposes because if you lose access to the root user, it would put you in trouble.

Though I have listed some important points, you will encounter other problems along the way. Remember that Google is a friend and the official forums are great when it comes to asking for help with each of those products. Happy coding! END

By: Vaibhav Kaushal

The author is a Web developer staying in Bengaluru who loves writing for technology magazines. He can be reached at *vaibhavkaushal123@gmail.com.*

Create Your First App
with Android Studio

Android Studio is a new Android development environment developed by Google. It is based on IntellJ IDEA, which is similar to Eclipse with the ADT plugin. Let's get familiar with the installation of Android Studio and some of the precautions that must be taken during installation.

Android is gaining market share and opening up new horizons for those who want to develop Android apps. Android app development doesn't require any investments because all the tools needed for it are free. It has been quite a while since Android app development began and most of us are aware of how things work. Just install Java, then install Eclipse, download the ADT (Android Development Toolkit) bundle, do a bit of configuration and you are all set to develop Android apps. Google provides us with a new IDE called Android Studio, which is based on IntellJ IDEA. It is different from Eclipse in many ways. The most basic difference is that you don't have to do any configuration like you would have to for Eclipse. Android Studio comes bundled with the Android ADT, and all you need to do is to point it to where Java is installed on your system. In this article, I will cover a few major differences between Android Studio and the Eclipse+ADT plugin methods. Android Studio is currently available as an 'easy access preview' or developer preview, so several features will not be available and there are chances that you may encounter bugs.

First, let's install Android Studio. I'm assuming yours is a Windows OS with pre-installed JDK as the developer machine's configuration. One thing to check is that the JDK version is later than version 6. Next, go to the link: *http://developer.android.com/sdk/installing/studio.html*. Here, you'll see the button for downloading Android Studio. The Web page automatically recognises your OS and provides you with the compatible version. If you need to download for some other OS, just click on 'Download for other Platforms' (refer to Figure 1). Once downloaded, you can follow the set-up wizard. There might be a few challenges. For example, at times, for Windows systems, the launcher script isn't able to find Java. So you need to set an environment variable called JAVA_HOME and point it to your JDK folder. If you are on Windows 8, you can follow these steps to set an environment variable: click on *Computer -> Properties -> Advanced System Settings -> Advanced Tab* (on the *System Properties Dialogue) -> Environment Variables*. Then, under *System Variables*, click on *New*.

Another problem might be the PATH variable. In the same manner as above, reach the *Environment Variable* dialogue box, and there, instead of creating a new variable, find the existing PATH variable and edit it. To the existing value, just add a semicolon at the end (if it's not already there) and add the path to the

Figure 1: Download Android Studio

Figure 2: Welcome screen

bin folder of the JDK. Also, please note that if you are working with a 64-bit machine, the path to JDK should be something like: *C:\Program Files\Java\jdk1.7.0_21* and not *C:\Program Files (x86)\Java\jdk1.7.0.* If you don't have it in the former location, it means that a 64-bit version of Java isn't installed on your system; so install that first.

Now that the set-up is complete, we can go ahead and directly launch the Android Studio. There is no need to download the ADT plugin and configure it. When you launch it, you can see the *Welcome* screen (refer to Figure 2), which is very powerful and deep. You can directly check out the Version Control Systems from the *Welcome* screen itself. The Version Control Systems supported are GitHub, CVS, Git, Mercurial and Subversion. Then, from the *Configure* menu within the *Welcome* screen, you can configure the SDK manager, plugins, import/export settings, project default settings and the overall settings for the IDE—all this without even launching the IDE. You can also access the *Docs* and the *How-Tos* from the *Welcome* screen. Next, the *New Project* screen is almost similar to what it looked like in Eclipse, but now there's no need to select Android Application or anything else. You are directly

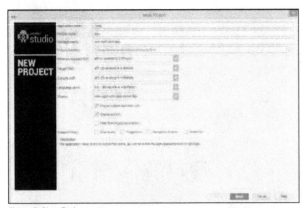

Figure 3: New Project

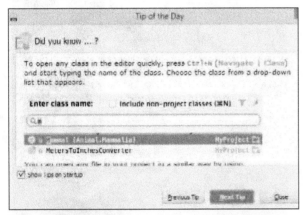

Figure 4: Tip of the day

Figure 5: Preview of different layouts

at the spot from where you can start off a new Android Project (refer to Figure 3). Among other interesting things about Android Studio is the 'Tip of the day' section (refer to Figure 4), which makes you familiar with the IDE.

Now, let's focus on some specific features that come with Android Studio (and quoting directly from the Android Developers Web page):

- Gradle-based build support.
- Android-specific refactoring and quick fixes.
- Lint tools to catch performance, usability, version compatibility and other problems.
- ProGuard and app-signing capabilities.

- Template-based wizards to create common Android designs and components.
- A rich layout editor that allows you to drag-and-drop UI components, preview layouts on multiple screen configurations, and much more.
- Built-in support for Google Cloud Platform, making it easy to integrate Google Cloud Messaging and App Engine as server-side components.

One of the major changes with respect to Eclipse is the use of Gradle. Previously, Android used Ant for build, but with Android Studio, this task has been taken over by Gradle. In last year's Google I/O, sources at Google had talked about the new Android build system –- Gradle. To quote from the Gradle website: "Google selected Gradle as the foundation of the Android SDK build system because it provides flexibility along with the ability to define common standards for Android builds. With Gradle, Android developers can use a simple, declarative DSL to configure Gradle builds supporting a wide variety of Android devices and App stores. With a simple, declarative DSL, Gradle developers have access to a single, authoritative build that powers both the Android Studio IDE and builds from the command-line." Owing to Gradle, people will also notice a change in the project structure as compared to the project structure in Eclipse. Everything now resides inside the SRC folder. But from a developer's perspective, it is essentially all still the same.

The other major, and rather useful, change is the ability to preview the layout on different screen sizes (refer to Figure 5, as shown during the Google I/O last year). While retaining the drag-and-drop designer function, the text mode has the preview pane to the right which allows for previewing the layout on various screen sizes. There is also an option for making a landscape variation design for the same app without having to do anything much on the code level.

This is just the tip of the iceberg, and the features discussed above are amongst the major changes in terms of build and layout designing. I would encourage zealous developers who want to try out this IDE to visit the Android developers' page and check out the Android Studio section. It is definitely a different way to approach Android app development, with the focus shifting towards development rather than configuration and management. END

By Manit Singh Kalsi

The author works as a mobile evangelist in the Mobility Center of Excellence at Genpact Headstrong Capital Markets. He is a Java and JavaScript developer who enjoys exploring new technologies and frameworks. When not coding, he is either strumming his guitar or playing video games. Follow him @manitsinghkalsi

Sandya Mannarswamy

In this month's column, we discuss natural language processing and its role in information retrieval.

In last month's column, we had discussed various compression schemes for maintaining the data structures associated with information retrieval systems. You will recall that the major tasks of the information retrieval (IR) systems are to process the user query, find documents that are potentially relevant to the user query and return a ranked result containing the retrieved documents. In other words, IR can be thought of as three major processes— query processing, matching (the query to the relevant documents in the collection) and ranking the results using certain heuristics so that the documents most relevant to the user are listed earlier in the results.

Earlier, we had discussed how user queries can be processed using tokenisation, stemming and lemmatisation techniques. For matching, we had discussed techniques such as the Boolean model of information retrieval, which performs the binary classification of documents as either relevant or irrelevant to the query; and the vector space model which assigns weightage with respect to the relevance of the document to the query under consideration. Ranking of retrieved results can be based on the weights associated with relevance, or through external techniques like page ranking, which ranks the results depending on how many authoritative page links there are to a particular page, etc.

While we described the complete cycle of information retrieval in terms of query processing, matching and ranking, we had not really used any semantic information contained either in the query or in the document itself to help the information retrieval process. Statistical properties such as Term Frequency-Inverse Document Frequency (TF-IDF) associated with terms in the document have been successfully used to build functional IR systems. However, such statistical techniques have their own drawbacks. For instance, if we compare how human beings would perform information retrieval techniques with automatic machine driven information retrieval, it is clear that human beings are more comfortable analysing the syntactic and semantic contents of the documents/queries to aid information retrieval. As an example, consider a simple query, "What are the foods that do not contain magnesium?" As human beings, we all know that we are looking for foods that do not contain magnesium. But try typing this query in Google, or any other search engine. You will find that most of them ignore the negation term and return you results featuring 'foods that contain magnesium,' 'whether eating magnesium is healthy,' 'how you can get enough magnesium,' etc?" The results returned by the search engine are absolutely useless to users because they are the very opposite of their information needs. If the same query is asked to a human being, such a mistake will never happen because the semantic meaning of the query is well understood by humans and, hence, they will only give details on which foods do not contain magnesium. Just doing a word matching or shallow parsing will not suffice in this case, since the word 'NOT' being a common word, it is typically dropped during the query processing itself. On the other hand, if natural language processing techniques are applied to query processing, such a mistake will not happen. Increasingly, information retrieval systems are adopting the use of natural language processing to improve their performance. In the next few columns, we will focus on natural language processing (NLP) and how it is useful in information retrieval systems.

NLP can be applied to the IR tasks of query processing, document matching and relevance ranking. Recall that document matching is done using our main data structures of the dictionary and inverted index. We had discussed using either single word tokens or multi-word tokens from the documents as terms representing the document, and we used these terms to represent the document in the inverted index. While single word tokens (unigrams) can be used directly, we had also considered bi-grams (two consecutive tokens) and trigrams (three consecutive tokens) to improve the matching between query and document. For example, if we had used only unigrams, then if the user searched for 'New York', the retrieved document set could include documents containing just 'New' and just 'York', and we would have to impose a post-processing step to filter out those documents where only one of the two unigrams are present, instead of both. On the other hand, a bi-gram representation of the term 'New York' in an inverted index would have allowed us to directly return only those documents which contained 'New York'. Note that bi-grams need to be maintained in addition to unigrams, since unigrams would still be needed to answer a query for 'York'. Note that a user query for 'Who is the new priest for the town of York?' should not return documents which contain the term 'New York'. Given that many of our information retrieval systems are based on the 'bag of words' model, which does not consider the order of words in the document or query, most of our IR systems would fail this test. On the other hand, consider an NLP analysis of the query which determines that the word 'new' in the query is an adjective to the noun 'priest' and is not part of the noun for 'York'; then the query can be processed to look for 'York' as a unigram instead of retrieving documents which contain both the words 'new' and 'York' without understanding the syntactic structure of the query. Query processing can be enhanced by NLP to consider the syntactic structure, and each word/term in the query can be tagged with additional metadata containing information about its grammatical structure as a noun, verb, etc.

The challenge is to figure out which bi-grams are useful to be represented in the dictionary and which are not. Maintaining all bi-grams (or all trigrams) consumes computation resources and memory. So IR systems typically only maintain a sub-set of all possible bi-grams over the dictionary. The set of bi-grams that are maintained in the dictionary are chosen depending on how frequently they occur in the document collection without understanding their syntax. Let us consider the query: 'buy prefabricated units.' Users may be looking for a document which contains information on where to buy prefabricated units. Now consider a document which contains the sentence, 'In the forest, they prefabricated units and put them up for temporary use.' In the user query, the bi-gram 'prefabricated units' is a noun phrase whereas in the document, the word 'prefabricated' is a verb. Without using linguistic techniques for syntax parsing, it is not possible to distinguish that the document containing the sentence with the bi-gram 'prefabricated units' is not relevant to the user query. On the other hand, it is possible to use a simple 'Part of Speech' (POS) tagger to tag the various terms in the query, and document and use the POS tags information to aid the matching process. Use of such linguistic techniques in query processing and document matching is made possible by means of NLP.

One of the important points to note is that users typically use nouns very frequently in queries. Therefore, identifying nouns in documents and queries can be quite useful in document retrieval. A well-known NLP technique, known as 'Named Entity Recognition', can be quite useful for this purpose. We will discuss how Named Entity Recognition is possible using natural language processing of text in our next column.

So far, we have been discussing examples of how NLP can be used to aid information retrieval. There are different levels in which NLP can be used for IR. At the morphological level, linguistic techniques can be used in tokenisation, for stemming. At the syntax level, NLP can be used to determine whether a term in a query is a noun or verb, using that information to improve matching. At the semantic level, NLP can be useful in identifying the intended meaning of a word based on the context to improve the matching process. Many of the documents are semi-structured. At the discourse level, it is possible to use the structure of the document to decide whether it is a fact or an opinion that is being reported. For instance, a scientific abstract could start by stating the facts and then conclude by stating the hypothesis it is proposing in the paper. By using the structure of the document to identify a paragraph as an abstract in the document, we can use it as a summary for the document also. At the pragmatic level, word knowledge which lies outside the document collection can be used to aid in query processing and document matching. For example, consider the sentence, 'I went to the bank and withdrew money.' Now, the

word 'bank' can represent the banks of the river or it can represent the place where financial dealings take place. The worldly knowledge that money can be withdrawn from a bank allows us to distinguish that the word 'bank' in this particular case refers to financial institutions (and, thereby, return documents pertaining to banks which facilitate financial transactions) and not to river banks. Thus, there are multiple levels at which NLP can aid IR. We will discuss this further in the next column.

We are all familiar with Twitter and how information is exchanged through short tweets. Here is a takeaway question for our readers. Given that one is interested in finding all relevant tweets related to a popular event or incident, how would you construct an information retrieval system for tweets?

My 'must-read book' for this month

This month's book suggestion comes from one of our readers, Kanthi, and her recommendation is very appropriate for this month's column. She recommends an excellent article on information retrieval titled, 'How Google finds your needle in the Web's haystack' by David Austin and it is available at: *http://www.ams.org/samplings/feature-column/fcarc-pagerank*. This article

provides a good description of the page rank algorithm employed by Google to rank the relevant results. Thank you, Kanthi, for sharing this link.

If you have a favourite programming book/article that you think is a must-read for every programmer, please do send me a note with the book's name, and a short write-up on why you think it is useful so I can mention it in the column. This would help many readers who want to improve their software skills.

If you have any favourite programming questions/software topics that you would like to discuss on this forum, please send them to me, along with your solutions and feedback, at *sandyasm_AT_yahoo_DOT_com*. Till we meet again next month, happy programming! END

By: Sandya Mannarswamy

The author is an expert in systems software and is currently working with Hewlett Packard India Ltd. Her interests include compilers, multi-core and storage systems. If you are preparing for systems software interviews, you may find it useful to visit Sandya's LinkedIn group 'Computer Science Interview Training India' at *http://www.linkedin.com/groups?home=HYPERLINK "http://www.linkedin.com/groups?home=&gid=2339182"&HYPERLINK "http://www.linkedin.com/groups?home=&gid=2339182"gid=2339182*

Be a Proficient Web 2.0 Developer!

This article walks readers through the requisites of a good Web developer. For those who wish to make a career as a Web developer, it is a must-read!

Like many scientific concepts, the term Web 2.0 doesn't have a clear definition or boundary, but encompasses several principles. Primarily, it positions the Web as a platform, as software as a service and not as a packaged product. Tim O'Reilly has explained Web 2.0 in his landmark article by comparing trends that define Web 2.0. The complete article 'What is Web 2.0, Designs and patterns for the next generation of software' is available on *http://oreilly.com/pub/a/web2/archive/what-is-web-20.html?page=1*

Lack of a clear boundary is evident in startups, too, where developers handle user queries, provision servers and other hardware, etc. It's not uncommon to see a PHP guru trying to tame a heavily swapping VPS, installing the latest HTTP load balancer, deploying code to servers and performing several other tasks. This convergence is called 'DevOps' and is the Web 2.0 way of doing things. Having a fluid boundary makes it extremely difficult to clearly define the responsibilities and skills of a Web 2.0 developer. Most developers have a multitude of skills.

They spend a large portion of their day (and night!) writing code, refactoring, trying out code snippets, checking out technology news, and helping other developers on various forums–thus constantly pitching themselves against similar, bigger and brighter minds on the Web.

If you yearn to be a Web 2.0 developer and wish to make a mark in an industry that is evolving rapidly, you should first know that the older ways of crafting solutions might not yield productive artefacts, and you require new methodologies and tools to architect and deliver solutions. You should be willing to invest time and energy in learning new things to keep up, otherwise you risk being outdated. You should constantly read, learn and continue to build your arsenal to be successful. The following sections should help you get started on your journey to becoming a successful Web 2.0 developer.

Hardware and other gear

You should have access to a laptop/PC (the older the better and even Celeron is fine!). Then you require an Internet connection with a wireless router if possible, because you'll need it to download applications and interact with other developers on various forums.

Operating system

Linux is a favourite among Web developers and most Web solutions, barring a few, are hosted on some flavour of Linux. So knowledge about Linux is a must for you to find your way around host machines. A good knowledge of the command line (CL) syntax is essential. And familiarity with *awk* and *sed* programming is an added advantage.

Centos and Ubuntu are two of the most popular distributions. The magazine that you are reading regularly distributes the latest versions of these OSs in the accompanying DVDs. You can also visit the website of a particular OS, to download its latest version.

Browse the following to know more:
- The community enterprise operating system - *http://www.centos.org*
- Ubuntu Desktop and Ubuntu Server – *http://www.ubuntu.com*
- An A-Z index of the bash command line for Linux - *http://ss64.com/bash/*
- 'Linux in a Nutshell', 6th Edition, by Ellen Siever, Stephen Figgins, Robert Love, Arnold Robbins, O'Reilly. This is a good desktop reference and should be part of your library.
- 'sed and awk pocket reference', 2nd Edition, by Arnold Robbins, O'Reilly.
- 'Classic Shell Scripting', 6th Edition, by Arnold Robbins, Nelson H F Beebe, O' Reilly

The database

Web 2 applications are much more than plain websites—they provide business functionality and require data and results to be stored. Knowledge of a database is a must for a Web 2 developer. As of writing this article, MySQL is the most popular choice for Web solutions. Postgres is beginning to gain widespread acceptance, while Percona (a MySQL clone) provides replication and other capabilities that are otherwise available only in the commercial offerings of MySQL. You could start with MySQL. A good knowledge of command line MySQL administration and phpMyAdmin is a must, not to mention a sound knowledge of writing SQL queries. Knowing database modelling using IDEF1X and being able to refactor the data models is an added advantage.

Browse the following to know more:
- Percona - *http://www.percona.com/*
- Postgres - *http://www.postgresql.org/*
- phpMyAdmin - *http://www.phpmyadmin.net*
- MySQL Developer Zone - *http://dev.mysql.com/*

- MySQL in a Nutshell, 6th Edition, by Russell J.T. Dyer, O'Reilly

Scripting

Knowledge of server side scripting is what distinguishes a Web 2 developer. Expertise in either PHP, Python, Ruby or Perl is a must. Though the relative advantages of each of them are debatable, there are several people who have started out with PHP. You might want to consider PHP before you move to other scripting languages. In addition to learning the syntax, a good grasp of the coding and naming conventions of the scripting language are a must for others to understand your code and help you when you seek their assistance.

Client side scripting using ECMA Script (or JavaScript, as it is popularly known) is essential to provide visual appeal to your applications. AJAX style scripting is something that you should learn, in order to make your pages truly interactive.

Browse the following to know more:
- PHP: Hypertext Preprocessor - *http://www.php.net/*
- Python programming language - *http://www.python.org/*
- Perl programming language - *http://www.perl.org/*
- Ruby, a programmer's best friend - *https://www.ruby-lang.org/en/*
- 'Programming PHP', 3rd Edition, by Kevin Tatroe, Peter MacIntyre and Rasmus Lerdof, O'Reilly
- 'Programming Perl', 4th Edition, by Tom Christiansen, Brian D Foy, Larry Wall and Jon Orwant, O'Reilly
- 'Programming Python', 4th Edition, by Mark Lutz, O'Reilly
- 'The Ruby Programming Language', 1st Edition, by David Flanagan and Yukihiro Matsumoto, O'Reilly

Markup and CSS

All content on the Web is rendered by a browser using HTML markup tags. A thorough knowledge of CSS and HTML is a must to bend and tweak your server side scripting to render your content aesthetically and include some fizz! It is an advantage if you are aware of at least one theme engine like PHPtemplate, PHPTAL, Smarty or XTemplate. Knowing the HTML and XML DOM models adds to making your resume stand out.

Browse the following to know more:
- PHP Template Attribute Language - *http://phptal.org/*
- Smarty Template Engine - *http://www.smarty.net/*
- PHP XTemplate - *http://www.phpxtemplate.org/ HomePage*
- Cascading Style Sheets - *http://www.w3.org/Style/CSS/*
- SASS – Syntactically Awesome Stylesheets - *http://sass-lang.com/*
- Compass – CSS Authoring Framework - *http://*

compass-style.org/
- Bootstrap - *http://getbootstrap.com/css/*
- The dynamic stylesheet language - *http://lesscss.org/*
- 'CSS: The Definitive Guide', 3rd Edition, by Eric A Meyer, O'Reilly

Frameworks and patterns

As the saying goes, "A good programmer knows what to write and a great programmer knows what to rewrite." So it's unlikely that you'll be asked to code a login page over and over again, especially when frameworks and software patterns are available for free. Being aware about the frameworks available for your scripting language is essential and a sound knowledge of at least one of them is a must.

Browse the following to know more:

- Zend Framework - *http://www.zend.com/en/products/framework/*
- CodeIgniter: A fully baked PHP framework - *http://ellislab.com/codeigniter*
- PEAR – PHP extension and application repository - *http://pear.php.net/*
- Django: The Web framework for perfectionists with deadlines - *https://www.djangoproject.com/*
- The Pylons Project - *http://www.pylonsproject.org/*
- JQuery: A feature-rich JavaScript library - *http://jquery.com/*
- Dojo: *http://dojotoolkit.org/*
- Mootools: A compact Javascript framework - *http://mootools.net/*
- Ruby on Rails: Web development that doesn't hurt - *http://rubyonrails.org/*
- 'Zend Framework, A Beginner's Guide', 1st Edition, by Vikram Vaswani, McGraw-Hill
- 'Zend Framework In Action', by Rob Allen, Nick Lo and Steven Brown, Manning
- 'Professional CodeIgniter', by Thomas Myer, Wrox
- 'Dojo: The Definitive Guide', 1st Edition, by Matthew A Russell, O'Reilly

HTTP servers

Apache is the Web server of choice for hosting Web applications. Knowing how it works is essential. To truly exploit its powers, get your hands dirty on the Apache directives.

NGINX is gaining popularity as a low memory footprint HTTP server for PHP and Perl applications using fast CGI. It can also be deployed as a HTTP load balancer.

Lighttpd is a lightweight HTTP server usually used to serve static content and complement the main HTTP server so that page downloads to the browser can be accelerated.

Browse the following to know more:

- Apache HTTP server - *http://projects.apache.org/*

projects/http_server.html
- NGINX - *http://nginx.org/*
- Lighttpd - *http://www.lighttpd.net/*
- 'Apache: The Definitive Guide', 3rd Edition, by Ben Laurie and Peter Laurie, O'Reilly

Architecture

To build industrial strength software applications, you'll need a sound architecture represented with an appropriate notation like IDEF1X or UML. As a programmer, you would be required to understand the rules conveyed in these architecture diagrams, which need to be built into the code. So a sound knowledge of IDEF1X and UML is a must. Further knowledge of the software architectural patterns is definitely an advantage.

To know more, read:

- 'Design Patterns: Elements of Reusable Object-Oriented Software', 3rd Edition, by Eric Gamma, Richard Helm, Ralph Johnson and John Vlissides, Addison-Wesley

Supporting disciplines

Software development has supporting disciplines like testing and versioning of the various artefacts. So a sound knowledge of automated testing and version control is essential to be a great software developer. Debugging is another skill that you should cultivate to fix your applications, so that they work the way they should.

Browse the following to know more:

- Concurrent Versions System - *http://www.nongnu.org/cvs/*
- Apache Subversion - *http://subversion.apache.org/*
- Git - *http://git-scm.com/*
- PHPUnit - *http://phpunit.sourceforge.net/*
- Firebug - *https://getfirebug.com/*
- Webdeveloper Toolbar - *http://chrispederick.com/work/web-developer/*

Regular expressions

Regular expressions (regex) are used extensively in programming to find patterns for replacement. In your career as a programmer, you will use regular expressions extensively in your programming and research. Most HTTP server redirect rules are based on regular expressions. For that matter, you may have used regular expressions unknowingly. Surprised? *.*, which is the notation for a file of any name and any extension, is the simplest example to illustrate the power of regex. So get yourself acquainted with regex for a truly fruitful experience.

Browse through:

- *'Mastering Regular Expressions'*, 3rd Edition, by Jeffrey E F Friedl, O'Reilly

Methodology

Developing software is difficult, and without a meaningful methodology it becomes both difficult and painful. Technology is solving newer and newer problems, and business models are being rewritten almost every three years. Remember Orkut was overshadowed by Hi5, and Hi5 was overshadowed by Facebook, as the social networking platform of choice, all within about five years. Such rapid changes require high velocity programming, which in turn, requires an agile method like Scrum or XP.

As software engineering continues to evolve, we are beginning to see the convergence of the 'development' and the 'operations' functions; so as a developer, you should be comfortable writing new code as well as fixing legacy ones even while answering questions on your support portal.

Browse through:
- Extreme Programming - *http://www.extremeprogramming.org/*
- Scrum - *https://www.scrum.org/*
- DevOps - *http://devops.com/*

Philosophy

It's true that programmers live and work adhering to a certain philosophy. You are likely to come across terms like the DRY Principle, Inversion of Control, etc. To make it easy for you to discover a work philosophy that suits your personality, it's highly recommended that you read the following essays to truly distinguish yourself.

Essays you must read:
- The Cathedral and the Bazaar, by Eric S Raymond - *http://www.catb.org/~esr/writings/cathedral-bazaar/cathedral-bazaar/*
- Beyond Code, by Rajesh Setty - *http://www.rajeshsetty.com/resources/books/beyond-code/*
- Mythical Manmonth, by Fredrick Brooks - *http://en.wikipedia.org/wiki/The_Mythical_Man-Month*

Copyright laws

As a programmer, and especially after you've read this article, you'll be tempted to try and reuse code as much as possible but this does come with some caveats. Usage of someone else's work requires their consent, and most of them advertise the terms of this consent by publishing their work under a set of copyright laws. So an awareness of the various licensing mechanisms like Creative Commons, Copy Left, BSD, etc, will ensure that you don't get on the wrong side of the law, and that you use the code according to the licence terms under which it has been released.

Business analysis

A project involves multiple stakeholders. You should learn the fine art of mapping business requirements to architectural diagrams and then translate these architectural diagrams to code. When this step is done right, fewer bugs reach the customer, and you spend less time dealing with a frustrated client. An understanding of the client's business is essential to achieve this.

Project management

Though you needn't know all the nuances of being a project manager, it is essential that you know how to prioritise tasks. You must know how these tasks are related to each other and how a delay in one critical task leads to the whole project being delayed. To be on top of the schedule you should be organised in your activities to ensure that everything works on the day of deployment. Choose the method that works for you. Here are a couple of books to get you started.

Browse through:
- Seven Habits of Highly Effective People, by Franklin Covey - *http://www.franklincovey.com/*
- Getting Things Done, by David Allen - *http://www.gtdtimes.com/*

Aesthetics

A thing of beauty is a joy for ever. Without an aesthetic appeal, a product is unlikely to find acceptance, no matter what features you put into it. Visual appeal in terms of colour, layout, typography, fonts and other eye candy is a must, and as a Web 2 programmer, this is an essential skill for your success.

Downloading code

There are several online repositories from where you can download code snippets or an entire project, and modify it to your heart's content (check the accompanying licence for restrictions).

The most popular among source code repositories are *https://github.com/* and *http://sourceforge.net/*. Check out the trending repositories on GitHub to see and participate in the most active projects. SourceForge has a 'hall of fame' called 'Project of the month'. Another notable mention is *http://freecode.com/* which was called 'Fresh Meat' a few years back. It has a list of the most popular projects. Google Code *(http://code.google.com/)* has several popular APIs and tools that you might find useful.

Keeping up with others by hanging out and networking

Most of the technologies mentioned above have well documented manuals and 'Getting started' guides. The forums on these sites are very active and responses to questions often get posted within a few seconds. There are several online sites that have presentation slides, speaker notes and videos that you can download for free. Check out Slideshare *(http://www.slideshare.net/)* and Slashdot *(http://slashdot.org/)*. Slashdot has all the news to whet your appetite for all things geeky.

You need to complement your quest for knowledge by hanging out with people of your own kind. So you have to 'flock' with 'birds of the same feather'. Most programmers exchange ideas and post queries on the several Stack Exchange sites *(http://stackexchange.com/)*. You'll be awarded points for accepting other people's answers for questions you have posted and answering other people's questions. You will most probably use two of the 100 odd sites out there – Server Fault *(http://serverfault.com)* and Stack Overflow *(http://stackoverflow.com)*. So register yourself for a Stack Exchange account, earn points, badges and see your reputation grow. Some Web development companies rely on this reputation score while evaluating job applications.

Hasgeek *(https://hasgeek.com/)* provides online discussion spaces for geeks and even hosts events. You can learn new things on these channels or if you feel confident enough, participate in their 'hacknights'. By the way, they do have a job portal.

IBM Developer Works has several tutorials that cover a broad technology landscape *(http://www.ibm.com/developerworks/)*. The articles on the site come in bite sizes and do not overwhelm the reader. It's a good place to begin your quest for knowledge.

For the latest on hardware–yes hardware, because remember, you write your software to run on some hardware – visit *http://www.anandtech.com/*. AnandTech has a review on most hardware that hits the market.

The magazine you are reading has an annual conference for open source enthusiasts called OSI Days. It offers tremendous opportunities to hear eminent open source programmers talk about their technologies, platforms and work.

Most cities have several special interest groups – Bar Camps, the Drupal Community and Linux Users Groups are some of the most popular ones. Join the ones that you find exciting and interact with people, seek help with your code, share ideas and watch yourself grow. END

By: Sridhar Pandurangiah

The author is the co-founder and director of Sastra Technologies, a start-up engaged in providing EDI solutions on the cloud. He can be contacted at: *sridhar@sastratechnologies.in /sridharpandu@gmail.com*. He maintains a technical blog at *sridharpandu.wordpress.com*

Anil Seth

Playing with Erlang Zotonic Modules

In continuation of earlier articles on Erlang Zotonic, let's now go through the stages of adding a chat module to the blog site that was created last month.

We begin by going a step beyond what was accomplished last month. Note that when you set up a running site in Zotonic, it is time to expand the site by using modules. One of the challenges is to see if you can make all the changes without needing to restart Zotonic.

As an example, let us select the chat module and look at adding it to the blog site.

Download the source from *http://code.google.com/p/zchat/*.

Installation and getting started

Start the Zotonic server and keep it running in a terminal window:

```
$ cd zotonic
$ ./start.sh
```

Download the zip file of the source from *http://code.google.com/p/zchat/source/browse/* and install it in the modules sub-directory of the blog site as follows, in a new terminal window:

```
$ cd zotonic/priv/sites/blogsite/modules
$ unzip Downloads/zchat-X.zip
$ mv zchat-X mod_chat
```

You need to enable this module from *http://blogsite:8000/admin/modules*. Locate the chat module and activate it. You will need a page and a dispatch rule to access chat.

In the directory *mod_chat/templates*, create a file *chat.tpl* with the following content:

```
{% extends "base.tpl" %}
{% block content %}
  {% include "_chat_box.tpl" %}
{% endblock %}
```

Now create a file *mod_chat/dispatch/dispatch* with the following content:

```
[
    {chat, ["chat"], controller_template, [{template, "chat.tpl"}]}]
```

```
]
```

From the Zotonic shell, give the command to reload the modules:

```
(zotonic001@myhost)1> z:m().
```

Browsing *http://blogsite:8000/chat* should display the form for chatting. If you open the same page on another browser, you will see two anonymous users and you can chat between the two browser sessions. You may open the same page on multiple tabs and all the sessions will be part of a group chat.

In case you want to have the option to chat from the home page, you will need to modify *home.tpl* to include '_chat_box.tpl'. You can easily include it in the content block. Or if you want to show it in the sidebar, the following lines should be added to *blogsite/template/home.tpl*:

```
{% block  sidebar %}
    {% include "_sidebar.tpl" %}
    {% include "_chat_box.tpl" %}
{% endblock %}
```

If you now browse *http://blogspot:8000/*, you should find the chat form in the sidebar. It may not look attractive but it works! Again, you can chat with other users on the home page. However, users on the chat page will not be able to chat with users on the home page. We will return to this a little later.

Usability

Since chatting with anonymous users is not particularly interesting, explore the list of modules and see if the usability can be improved.

The authentication module is already enabled. If you look at the dispatch rules for this module (see file *zotonic/modules/mod_authentication/dispatch/dispatch*), you will find that the two paths needed are */logon* and */logoff*.

You may activate the 'Signup users' module so that the users can create their accounts. The path for this module is */signup*. Signup requires verification via email, by default. You can disable it by setting *mod_signup.request_confirm* to *false*. You will need to edit the *zotonic/config* file for that.

The last few lines will then become:

```
%% Page length
{pagelen, 5},
{mod_signup, [{request_confirm, false}]}
].
```

You will now need to reload the modules from the Zotonic shell:

```
(zotonic001@myhost)2> z:m().
```

You can directly go to pages */signup, /logon* or */logoff* and try them. Now, you are ready to add them to the menu on the *navbar*. As an administrator, choose the option *Content -> Menu*. Now, go through the following steps:

1. Add menu item.
2. Choose 'New Page'. Select the name 'Signup' and, for convenience, select 'Page menu' as the category. Select the 'Published' option. Then 'Make' the page.
3. Edit the *Signup* menu option.
4. Click on 'Visit full editpage'.
5. In 'Advanced settings', give the page path as '/signup' and the unique name as 'signup' (same as in the dispatch rule). Save your choices.

Similarly, you can add the menu options for logging on and off. These options would then be visible on the navigation bar. Caution: The signup and logon options are silently ignored if you are already signed in.

You can experiment by creating users and signing in from different browsers.

Changing the chat code

You would have noticed that a user signed in on the home page is not visible to the user signed in to the */chat page*. View the *mod_chat/mod_chat.erl* file. Each submission of a chat message is handled by the event function.

The module also implements the behaviour of the *gen_server* module (see *'erl -man gen_server'* for details). This means that the module implements functions like *handle_call, handle_cast*, etc, which are implicitly called by the server.

The event function receives the chat message and notifies the Zotonic server, which will call *handle_cast* with appropriate parameters. Viewing the extract from the *handle_cast* function, you will find that the messages are sent to the list *ChatBoxes2*, which is the list of users signed into chat from the same room. The relevant code lines are:

```
handle_cast({{chat_done, Chat}, Ctx}, State) ->
    case State#state.chat_boxes of
        [] -> nop,
```

```
        {noreply, State};
    ChatBoxes ->
        ChatBoxes1 = [ X || X <- ChatBoxes, check_
process_alive(X#chat_box.pid, Ctx)],
        [ChatBox] = [ X || X <- ChatBoxes1, X#chat_box.
pid == Ctx#context.page_pid ],
        ChatBoxes2 = [ X || X <- ChatBoxes1, X#chat_box.
room=:=ChatBox#chat_box.room],
    ...
            [F(P) || #chat_box{pid=P} <- ChatBoxes2]
```

Delete the definition of ChatBoxes2 and replace the last line by

```
[F(P) || #chat_box{pid=P} <- ChatBoxes1]
```

In addition, first time a new chat window is displayed, the function handle_call is executed. Relevant function is:

```
handle_call({{add_chat_box, ChatBox}, Ctx}, _From, State) ->
    ChatBoxes = [ X || X <- [ChatBox|State#state.chat_boxes],
check_process_alive(X#chat_box.pid, Ctx)],
    ChatBoxes1 = [ X || X <- ChatBoxes, X#chat_box.room=:=z_
context:get_req_path(Ctx)],
    %% add new chat box to all
    render_userlist_row([{name, ChatBox#chat_box.name},
{upid, format_pid_for_html(ChatBox#chat_box.pid)}],
ChatBoxes1, Ctx),
    %% add existing chat boxes to new
    [ render_userlist_row([{name, CBox#chat_box.name}, {upid,
format_pid_for_html(CBox#chat_box.pid)}], [ChatBox], Ctx) ||
CBox <- tl(ChatBoxes1) ],
    {reply, ok, State#state{chat_boxes=ChatBoxes}};
```

In this case, ChatBoxes is the list of all chat sessions that are still alive and ChatBoxes1 is the subset of chat sessions that are on the same room. You can delete the definition of ChatBoxes1 and replace the references to it by ChatBoxes.

Now, run *z:m()* from the Zotonic shell. All chat sessions should now be visible.

This was just a simple change to illustrate the possibilities. A useful exercise would be to change the subject of chat in each room, with each user entering a particular room to chat with others in that room on a particular topic. Try it as an exercise.

The nice thing is that there was no downtime in all these experiments—not once was a restart of Zotonic needed. **END**

By: Anil Seth

The author has earned the right to do what interests him. You can find him online at *http://sethanil.com, http://sethanil. blogspot.com*, and reach him via email at *anil@sethanil.com*

Be Cautious While Using
Bit Fields for Programming

In this article, the author tells embedded C programmers why writing code involving bit fields needs to be done carefully, failing which the results may not be as expected. However, bit fields are handy as they involve only low level programming and result in efficient data storage.

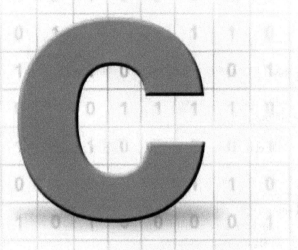

Embedded C programmers who have worked with structures should also be familiar with the use of bit fields structures. Use of bit fields is one of the key optimisation methods in embedded C programming, because these allow one to pack together several related entities, where each set of bits and single bits can be addressed. Of course, the usage of bit fields is 'easy' and comes handy, especially during low level programming. Though considered as one of the unique features of C programming, bit fields do have some limitations. Let us look at these by exploring the example problems in this article.

Data types and bit fields

Let us look into the signed qualifiers affecting the output of the bit field structure. Please note that the code snippets provided here are tested with the GCC compiler [gcc version 4.7.3] running under a Linux environment.

Let us consider a simple small C code snippet as shown below, with a structure named *bit field*, with three integer fields—*hours*, *mins* and *secs*, of bit field sizes 5, 6 and 6, respectively:

```
typedef struct bit_field
{
    int hours : 5;
    int mins : 6;
    int secs : 6;
}time_t;
```

Now let us declare a variable *alarm* of *type time_t* and set values as 22, 12 and 20, respectively:

```
//Declaration of the variable of type time_t
time_t alarm;
/Assigning the values to the different members of the bit-
field structures
alarm.hours = 22;
alarm.mins  = 12;
alarm.secs  = 20;
```

When we print these values using a simple *printf* statement, what could be the output? At first, most of us will envision the answers to be 22, 12 and 20, for *hours*, *mins* and *secs* respectively. Whereas when we actually compile and run the run the code, the value printed for the hours would be different - 10, 12 and 20 (as shown in Figure 1).

Where did we go wrong?

1. We all know that the default signed qualifier for the 'int' is 'signed int'.
2. We reserved 5 bits for storing the *hours field* assuming we were using the 24-hour format. From among 5 bits, 1 bit was used for storing the sign of the number, which means only 4 bits were then available for storing the actual value. In these 4 bits, we can store the numbers ranging from -16 to +15 according to the formula (-2^k) to $([+2^k] -1)$ including '0', where 'k' indicates the number of bits.

Figure 1: Actual output

3. We will see how 22 is stored in binary form in 5 bits through pictorial representation (Figure 2).
4. From the table(as shown in Figure 2), it is very clear that sign bit (b4) is SET, which indicates the value is negative. So, when printed using the *printf* statement, we will get -10 (the decimal value of 10110), because of which we got an unexpected output.

Now that we have understood the problem, how do we fix it? It is very simple; just qualify 'int' to 'unsigned int' just before the hours in the bit field structure, as shown below. The corrected output is shown in Figure 3.

```
#include <stdio.h>
typedef struct bit_field
{
    unsigned int hours  : 5;
    unsigned int mins   : 6;
    unsigned int secs   : 6;
}time_t;
int main()
{
        //Declaration of the variable of type time_t
        time_t alarm;
        //Assigning the values to the different members of
the bit-field structures
        alarm.hours = 22;
        alarm.mins  = 12;
        alarm.secs  = 20;
        printf("Hours : %d\nMins : %d\nSecs : %d\n", alarm.
hours, alarm.mins, alarm.secs);
}
```

Bit wise operators definitely provide advantages, but they need to be used a 'bit' carefully. In the embedded programming environment, they might lead to major issues in case they are not handled properly.

Endianess of the architecture and bit fields

In this problem, we will see how Endianess affects the bit fields. Bit fields in C always start at Bit 0, which is the least significant bit (LSB) on Little Endian. But most compilers on Big Endian systems inconveniently consider the most significant bit (MSB)—Bit 0.

Note: Big Endian machines pack bit fields from the most significant byte to the least significant.

Little Endian machines pack bit fields from the least significant byte to the most.

To start with, let us consider the code(Labelled as *byte_order.c*) given below:

```
1 #include <stdio.h>
2 typedef union {
3        unsigned int value;
4        struct {
5                unsigned char one    : 8;
6                unsigned char two    : 8;
7                unsigned char three  : 8;
8                unsigned char four   : 8;
9        } bit_field;
10 } data_t;
11
12 int main() {
13
14        data_t var = {0x1A1B1C1D};
15        unsigned char *ptr = (unsigned char *)(&var);
16
17        printf("The entire hex value is 0x%X\n", var.
value);
18        printf("The first byte is 0x%X @ %p\n", *(ptr +
0), ptr + 0);
19        printf("The second byte is 0x%X @ %p\n", *(ptr +
1), ptr + 1);
20        printf("The third byte is 0x%X @ %p\n", *(ptr +
2), ptr + 2);
21        printf("The fourth byte is 0x%X @ %p\n", *(ptr +
3), ptr + 3);
22
23        return 0;
24 }
```

b4	b3	b2	b1	b0
1	0	1	1	0

Figure 2: Pictorial representation of the binary value of 22 in 5 bits

Figure 3: Correct output after correct usage of the data type

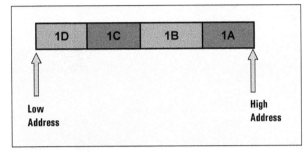

Figure 4: Output of the code *byte_order.c*

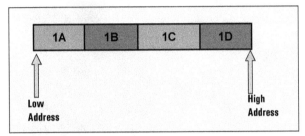

Figure 5: Byte-ordering in a Little–Endianess machine

Figure 6: Byte-ordering in a Big–Endianess machine

```
15        data_t var ;
16        unsigned char *ptr = (unsigned char*)(&var);
17        var.bit.v1   = 1;
18        var.bit.v2   = 2;
19        var.bit.v3   = 3;
20        var.bit.v4   = 4;
21        var.bit.v5   = 5;
22
23        printf("The Entire hex value is 0x%X\n", var.
value);
24        printf("The first byte is 0x%X @ %p\n", *(ptr +
0), ptr + 0);
25        printf("The second byte is 0x%X @ %p\n", *(ptr +
1), ptr + 1);
26
27        return 0;
28 }
```

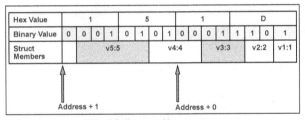

Figure 7: Output of the code *bit_order.c*

Hex Value		1				5				1				D	
Binary Value	0	0	0	1	0	1	0	1	0	0	0	1	1	1	0	1
Struct Members			v5:5					v4:4				v3:3		v2:2	v1:1	

Address + 1   Address + 0

Figure 8: Bit ordering in small Endianess architecture

When I run this code in my system, I get the output shown in Figure 4.

From Figure 4, it is very clear that the underlying architecture is following the little Endian. When the same code is run under a different architecture, which follows Big Endian, the result will be different. So, portability issues need to be considered while using bit fields.

Let's look at one more example to understand how bits are packed in Big Endian and Little Endian.

To start with, let us consider the sample code(Labelled as *bit_order.c*) given below:

```
1 #include <stdio.h>
2 typedef union {
3        unsigned short value;
4        struct {
5                unsigned short v1   : 1;
6                unsigned short v2   : 2;
7                unsigned short v3   : 3;
8                unsigned short v4   : 4;
9                unsigned short v5   : 5;
10       } bit;
11 } data_t;
12
13 int main() {
14
```

When I run this code in my system, I get the output as shown in Figure 7.

From this figure, one can see that the bits are packed from the least significant on a little Endian machine. Figure 8 helps us understand how the bits ordering takes place.

If you run the same code in big Endian architecture, you will get the output given in Figure 9.

For more clarity, see Figure 10.

From the last two examples, it is very clear that bit fields pose serious portability issues. When the same programs are compiled on *different* systems, they may not *work* properly. This is because some C compilers use the left-to-right order, while other C compilers use the right-to-left order. They also have architecture-specific bit orders and packing issues.

As a concluding note, let us list the advantages and limitations of bit fields structures.

Advantages

1. Efficiency - Storage of data structures by packing.

The entire hex value is : 0xCD0A
The first byte is 0xCD @ XXXX
The second byte is 0x0A @ YYYY

Note:
XXXX & YYYY are some addresses

Figure 9: Expected output of the code *bit_order.c* when run in big Endian architecture

Figure 10: Bit ordering in big Endianess architecture

2. Readability - Members can be easily addressed by the names assigned to them.
3. Low level programming – The biggest advantage of bit fields is that one does not have to keep track of how flags and masks actually map to the memory. Once the structure is defined, one is completely abstracted from the memory representation as in the case of bit-wise operations, during which one has to keep track of all the shifts and masks.

Limitations

1. As we saw earlier, bit fields result in non-portable code. Also, the bit field length has a high dependency on word size.
2. Reading (using *scanf*) and using pointers on bit fields is not possible due to non-addressability.
3. Bit fields are used to pack more variables into a smaller data space, but cause the compiler to generate additional code to manipulate these variables. This results in an increase in both space as well as time complexities.

4. The *sizeof()* operator cannot be applied to the bit fields, since *sizeof()* yields the result in bytes and not in bits. END

By: Satyanarayana Sampangi

The author is a member of the embedded software team at Emertxe Information Technologies *(http://www.emertxe.com)*. His area of interest lies in embedded C programming combined with data structures and microcontrollers. He likes to experiment with C programming in his spare time to explore new horizons. He can be reached at *satya@emertxe.com*

MongoDB: The Most Popular NoSQL Database

Here are the basics of MongoDB, the database used by thousands of organisations, including 30 of the top 100 companies in the world. Many of the world's most innovative Web companies use MongoDB.

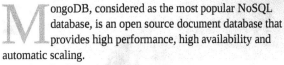

MongoDB, considered as the most popular NoSQL database, is an open source document database that provides high performance, high availability and automatic scaling.

It has the following key features.

High performance: MongoDB provides high performance data persistence. In particular, its support for embedded data models reduces I/O activity on database systems. Its indexes support faster queries and can include keys from embedded documents and arrays.

High availability: To ensure high availability, MongoDB has the replication facility (also called replica sets), which provides the following:
- Automatic failover
- Data redundancy

A replica set is a group of MongoDB servers that maintain the same data, providing redundancy and increasing data availability.

Automatic scaling: MongoDB provides horizontal scalability as part of its core functionality. Automatic sharding distributes data across a cluster of machines. Replica sets can provide eventually-consistent reads for low-latency high throughput deployments.

Installing MongoDB

MongoDB can be installed on various OSs in the following manner.

Red Hat
- Create a */etc/yum.repos.d/mongodb.repo* file to hold the following configuration information for the MongoDB repository:

```
[mongodb]
name=MongoDB Repository
baseurl=http://downloads-distro.mongodb.org/repo/redhat/os/
x86_64/
gpgcheck=0
enabled=1
```

- Install the MongoDB packages and associated tools as follows:

```
sudo yum install mongodb-org
```

Ubuntu
- Import the public key used by the package management system:

```
sudo apt-key adv --keyserver hkp://keyserver.ubuntu.com:80
--recv 7F0CEB10
```

Create the */etc/apt/sources.list.d/mongodb.list* list file using the following command:

```
echo 'deb http://downloads-distro.mongodb.org/repo/ubuntu-
```

```
upstart dist 10gen' | sudo tee /etc/apt/sources.list.d/
mongodb.list
```

- Reload the local package database:

```
sudo apt-get update
```

- Install the MongoDB packages:

```
sudo apt-get install mongodb-org
```

Debian
- Import the public key used by the package management system:

```
sudo apt-key adv --keyserver hkp://keyserver.ubuntu.com:80
--recv 7F0CEB10
```

Create the */etc/apt/sources.list.d/mongodb.list* list file using the following command:

```
echo 'deb http://downloads-distro.mongodb.org/repo/ubuntu-
upstart dist 10gen' | sudo tee /etc/apt/sources.list.d/
mongodb.list
```

- Reload the local package database:

```
sudo apt-get update
```

- Install the MongoDB packages:

```
sudo apt-get install mongodb-org
```

Getting started with MongoDB
From a system prompt, start MongoDB by running the 'mongo' command, as follows:

```
mongo
```

Select a database
From the Mongo shell, display the list of databases, with the following operation:

```
show dbs
```

Switch to a new database named *mydb*, with the following operation:

```
use mydb
```

> **Note:** If 'mydb' is not present, a database with the name 'mydb' will be created.

Confirm that your session has the *mydb* database as context, by checking the value of the *db* object, which returns the name of the current database, as follows:

```
Db
```

Create a collection and insert documents
A collection can be created and documents can be inserted by the following methods.
Using Python PyMongo:

```
Install Pymongo
sudo pip install pymongo

python
>>>import pymongo
>>> client = MongoClient()
>>> db = client.test_database
>>> collection = db.test_collection
>>> db.test_database.insert(({'i': i} for i in
xrange(10000)))
```

Directly from the Mongo shell:

```
for (var i = 1; i <= 25; i++) db.testData.insert( { x : i } )

or

j = { name : "mongo" }
k = { x : 3 }
db.testData.insert( j )
db.testData.insert( k )
```

Display collections

```
show collections
```

Or...

```
db.getCollectionNames()
```

MongoDB replication
In order to replicate the database, the following steps may be taken:
- Edit the */etc/mongodb.conf* on all the servers and add the following commands:

```
replSet=<Replication set name>
rest=true
```

- Start *mongod* with *mongod.conf* :

```
mongod -f /etc/mongodb.conf
```

- On the master MongoDB, enter the following command:

```
mongo
rs.initiate()
rs.add("<hostname/IP of slave>:<port number on which Mongo
is running, by default it runs on 27017>")
```

- On the slave MongoDB, enter the following command:

```
mongo
rs.initiate()
```

> **Note:** If there are an even number of slaves, it's advisable to add an arbiter to the setup. An arbiter is needed as a secondary cannot vote for itself; so, sometimes a situation arises when the votes are tied.

- Start the arbiter. Install MongoDB. Create the arbiter data directory *mkdir -p /data/arb* (this can be anything you want). Start the arbiter service:

```
mongod --port 3000 --dbpath /data/arb/ --replset
<replication set name used>
```

- Enter the following command on the master MongoDB to add the arbiter to the setup:

```
mongo

rs.addArb("<hostname/IP of arbiter>:3000")
```

- Use *rs.status()* to display the status of the replication set
- Another way of checking for the members in replica is to use the URL *http://<machine-name>:<port>/_replSet*

> **Note:** The port number is 1000 ahead of the MongoDB port; for example, if the Mongo port is 27017, here the port will be 28017.

Sharding

The config server processes are *mongod* instances that store the cluster's metadata. You designate a *mongod* as a config server using the *–configsvr* option. Each config server stores a complete copy of the cluster's metadata. In production deployments, you must deploy exactly three config server instances, each running on different servers to ensure good uptime and data safety. In test environments, you can run all three instances on a single server.

Steps to add sharding to the current setup

- Install MongoDB as described earlier.
- Create data directories for each of the three config server instances. By default, a config server stores its data files in the */data/configdb* directory. You can choose

a different location. To create a data directory, run a command similar to the following:

```
mkdir -p /data/configdb
```

- Start the config server instances as follows:

```
mongod --configsvr --dbpath /data/configdb --port 22019(you
can use any port)
```

- Start the *mongos* instance. The *mongos* instances are lightweight and do not require data directories. You can run a *mongos* instance on a system that runs other cluster components, such as on an application server or a server running a *mongod* process.

```
mongos --configdb <config server hostnames/IP>
```

Add shards to the cluster

- On the primary Mongo, issue the following command:

```
mongo --host <hostname of machine running mongos> --port
<port mongos listens on>
```

- On the *mongos* shell got by the above command, enter the following command:

```
sh.addShard( "<replication set name>/<Mongo
server1>:<port>,<Mongo server2>:<port>,<Mongo
server3>:<port>" )
```

Enable sharding for the database:

```
sh.enableSharding("<Name of the database you need to
shard")
```

Now check the sharding status:

```
mongo
use admin
db.printShardingstatus()
```

You can enable sharding for a collection as follows:
- Determine what you will use for the shard key.
- If the collection already contains data, you must create an index on the shard key using *ensureIndex()*. If the collection is empty, then MongoDB will create the index as part of the *sh.shardCollection()* step.
- Enable sharding for a collection by issuing the *sh.shardCollection()* method in the Mongo shell. The method uses the following syntax:

```
sh.shardCollection("<database>.<collection>", shard-key-
pattern selected above)
```

Some errors with MongoDB

A list of a few possible errors with MongoDB, along with solutions to them, is given below.

Error 1: Couldn't connect to server *127.0.0.1 shell/mongo.js:84* while starting Mongo shell.

Solution: This error takes place when Mongo is not shut down properly and the solution is as follows:

```
sudo rm /var/lib/mongodb/mongod.lock
sudo -u mongodb mongod -f /etc/mongodb.conf --repair
sudo start mongodb
```

Error 2: In a replication setup, the primary server goes down and the secondary server fails to became primary. All we have is just secondary.

Solution A

```
--Increase priority of a server so that arbiter chooses it
for primary
cfg = rs.conf() -Keep in mind the id
cfg.members[0].priority = 0.5
cfg.members[1].priority = 0.5
cfg.members[2].priority = 1
rs.reconfig(cfg)
```

Solution B

```
--Increase votes of a server so that arbiter chooses it for
primary
cfg = rs.conf() -Keep in mind the id
cfg.members[0].voting = 0.5
cfg.members[1].voting = 0.5
cfg.members[2].voting = 1
rs.reconfig(cfg)
```

Error 3: Child process failed; exited with error number 100.
Solution:

```
mongod --smallfiles
add nojournal = true to /etc/mongodb.conf
```

Error 4: Want to remove server from replication set.
Solution: Edit the */etc/mongodb.conf* file and delete the entry *repSet=<replication name>*. On the Mongo shell, enter *use local db.dropDatabase()*. Restart Mongo service. On the master Mongo, enter *rs.remove ("<Hostname/IP of the server:port")* END

By: Anand Patil

This FOSS enthusiast has six years of Linux experience and currently works as a senior automation consultant. You can reach him at *anandppatil83@yahoo.com*.

Getting Started with Hadoop on Windows

This introduction to Hadoop will tell you how to install and configure it in Windows. The prerequisites, the associated software and other requirements are all listed here, and there's advice on the dos and don'ts for a successful installation.

Hadoop is an Apache open source software library written completely in Java, designed to deliver a distributed file system (HDFS) and a method for distributed computation called MapReduce. It can scale up from single servers to thousands of machines.

It provides a framework that allows distributed processing of large sets of data across clusters of computers using simple programming models.

Hadoop implements MapReduce, which runs in two phases: the map phase and the reduce phase. The input to these computations is the data set of key/pair values. In short, the application is divided into many small fragments, each of which may be assigned to the map task. These map tasks are distributed and executed on any node in the cluster. If the nodes fail during the computation process, the tasks assigned to them are redistributed among the remaining nodes.

The Apache Hadoop project includes the following modules:
Hadoop Common: The common utilities that support the other Hadoop modules.
Hadoop Distributed File System (HDFS): A distributed file system that provides high-throughput access to application data.
Hadoop Yarn: A framework for job scheduling and cluster resource management.
Hadoop MapReduce: A yarn-based system for parallel processing of large data sets.

Hadoop deployment methods
Here is a list of the methods used to deploy Hadoop.
Standalone: In this mode, there are no daemons running; everything runs as in a single JVM. This mode is suitable for running the MapReduce program during development, as it is easy to test and debug.
Pseudo-distributed: The Hadoop daemon process runs on a local machine simulating a cluster on a small scale.
Fully distributed: Here, Hadoop runs on a cluster of machines providing a production environment.

This article focuses on introducing Hadoop, and deploying single-node pseudo-distributed Hadoop on a Windows platform.

Prerequisite software or tools for running Hadoop on Windows
You will need the following software to run Hadoop on Windows.

Supported Windows OSs: Hadoop supports Windows Server 2008 and Windows Server 2008 R2, Windows Vista and Windows 7. For installation purposes we are going to make use of Windows 7 Edition and JDK.

As Hadoop is written in Java, we will need to install Oracle JDK 1.6 or higher. Download Java from the link given in References [1] at the end of this article, and install it to the default location.

Windows SDK: Download and install Windows SDK 7 from the link given in References [2]. Windows SDK provides the tools, compilers, headers and libraries that are necessary to run Hadoop.

Cygwin: Hadoop requires UNIX command line tools like Cygwin or GnuWin32. Download and install Cygwin from the link given in References [3], to its default location *C:\cygwin64* and make sure to select the 'openssh' package and its associated prerequisites from the *Select packages* tab.

Maven and the Protocol buffer: Install Maven 3.0 or later and the Protocol buffer 2.5.0 into the *C:\maven* and *C:\protobuff* directories, respectively.

Setting environment variables

Navigate to *System properties---> Advanced ---> Environment Variables*. Add environment variables *JAVA_HOME, M2_HOME (for Maven)* and *Platform* (x64 or Win32 depending on the system architecture).

Note that the variable name, Platform, is case sensitive and values will be *x64* or *Win32* for 64-bit and 32-bit systems. Edit the path variable under *System variables* to add the following: *C:\cygwin64\ bin;C:\cygwin64\usr\sbin;C:\maven\bin; C:\protobuf*

The dos and don'ts

Given below are some of the issues usually faced while installing Hadoop on Windows.

If the JAVA_HOME environment variable is set improperly, Hadoop will not run. Set environment variables properly for JDK, Maven, Cygwin and Protobuffer. If you still get a 'JAVA_HOME not set properly' error, then edit the *C:\hadoop\bin\hadoop-env.cmd* file, locate 'set *JAVA_HOME =*' and provide the JDK path (with no spaces).

Do not use the Hadoop binary, as it is bereft of *Windowsutils. exe* and some *Hadoop.dll* files. Native IO is mandatory on Windows and without it the Hadoop installation will not work on Windows. Instead, build from the source code using Maven. It will download all the required components.

Download Hadoop from the link in References [4]. Building from the source code requires an active Internet connection the first time.

Building and configuring Hadoop on Windows

Select *Start ---> All Programs ---> Microsoft Windows SDK v7.1* and open the Windows SDK 7 command prompt as the administrator. Change the directory to *C:\hadoop* (if it doesn't exist, create it). Run the command prompt:

```
C:\Program Files\Microsoft SDKs\Windows\v7.1>cd c:\hadoop
C:\hadoop>mvn package -Pdist,native-win -DskipTests -Dtar
```

Note: The above step requires an active Internet connection because Maven will download all the dependencies. A successful build will generate a native binary package *C:\ hadoop\hadoop-dist\target\hadoop-2.2.0.tar.gz* directory. Extract hadoop-2.2.0.tar.gz under *C:\hdp*.

Starting a single node installation: If the build is successful, check out which Hadoop version by running the following command:

```
C:\hadoop>hadoop version
```

Startup scripts: The *C:\hdp\bin* directory contains the scripts used to launch Hadoop DFS and MapReduce daemons.

start-dfs.cmd: Starts the Hadoop DFS daemons, the namenode and datanode.

start-mapred.cmd: Starts the Hadoop MapReduce daemons, the jobtracker and tasktrackers.

start-all cmd: Starts all Hadoop daemons, the namenode, datanode, the jobtracker and tasktrackers.

start-dfs.cmd: Starts the Hadoop DFS daemons, the namenode and datanode. Use this before *start-mapred.sh*

start-mapred.cmd: Starts the Hadoop MapReduce daemons, the jobtracker and tasktrackers.

start:all.cmd - Starts all Hadoop daemons, the namenode, datanode, the jobtracker and tasktrackers.

The following section contains details on how to configure Hadoop on Windows. Assuming the install directory is *C:\ hdp*, run the command *C:\hadoop> cd C:\hdp\etc\hadoop*

Edit the file *hadoop-env.cmd* (which contains the environment variable settings used by Hadoop) in Notepad++ and add the following lines at the end of the file. Run the command prompt:

```
set HADOOP_PREFIX=c:\hdp
set HADOOP_CONF_DIR=C:\hdp\etc\hdp
set YARN_CONF_DIR=C:\hdp\etc\hadoop
set PATH=%PATH%;C:\hdp\bin
```

Before we get started with setting Hadoop environment variables and running Hadoop daemons, we need to configure the following files: *core-site.xml, hdfs-site.xml, yarn-site. xml mapred-site.xml* and the slave files located in *C:\hdp\etc\ hadoop*. The minimum configuration settings are given below.

Edit or create the file *C:\hdp\etc\hadoop\core-site.xml* (all Hadoop services and clients use this file to locate namenode; it contains the name of the default file system) and make sure it has the following configuration key:

```
<configuration>
<property>
<name>fs.defaultFS</name>
<value>hdfs://localhost:9000</value>
</property>
</configuration>
```

Edit or create the file *C:\hdp\etc\hadoop\hdfs-site. xml* (HDFS services use this file and it contains HTTP addresses for namenode and datanode) and add the following configuration key:

Figure 1: Working dfs format

Figure 2: HDP namenode and datanode

```
<configuration>
<property>
<name>dfs.replication</name>
<value>1</value>
</property>
<property>
<name>dfs.namenode.name.dir</name>
<value>file:/hdp/data/dfs/namenode</value>
</property>
<property>
<name>dfs.datanode.data.dir</name>
<value>file:/hdp/data/dfs/datanode</value>
</property>
</configuration>
```

Note that if namenode and datanode directories in the path C:\hdp\data\dfs\ are not present, you must create them.

Edit or create the file *C:\hdp\etc\hadoop\slaves*. (This file lists the hosts, one per line, where the Hadoop slave daemon's datanode and tasktrackers will run. By default, this contains the single entry localhost.) Make sure it has the following entry:

```
localhost
```

Edit or create *C:\hdp\etc\hadoop\mapred-site.xml* (contains the framework for executing MapReduce jobs) and add the following entries:

```
<configuration>
<property>
<name>mapreduce.framework.name</name>
<value>yarn</value>
</property>
</configuration>
```

Finally, edit or create *yarn-site.xml* and add the following entries:

```
<configuration>
<property>
<name>yarn.nodemanager.aux-services</name>
<value>mapreduce_shuffle</value>
</property>
<property>
<name>yarn.nodemanager.aux-services.mapreduce.shuffle.class</name>
<value>org.apache.hadoop.mapred.ShuffleHandler</value>
</property>
<property>
<name>yarn.application.classpath</name>
<value>
%HADOOP_HOME%\etc\hadoop,
%HADOOP_HOME%\share\hadoop\common\*,
%HADOOP_HOME%\share\hadoop\common\lib\*,
%HADOOP_HOME%\share\hadoop\mapreduce\*,
%HADOOP_HOME%\share\hadoop\mapreduce\lib\*,
%HADOOP_HOME%\share\hadoop\hdfs\*,
%HADOOP_HOME%\share\hadoop\hdfs\lib\*,
%HADOOP_HOME%\share\hadoop\yarn\*,
%HADOOP_HOME%\share\hadoop\yarn\lib\*
</value>
</property>
</configuration>
```

Initialising environment variables

Once all four files are configured, run *hadoop-env.cmd* and format the namenode file system. Run the following command prompt:

```
C:\hdp\etc\hadoop>hadoop-env.cmd
C:\hdp\etc\hadoop>C:\hdp\bin\hdfs namenode -format
```

Figure 3: HDP Yarn

Figure 4: Working Resource Manager

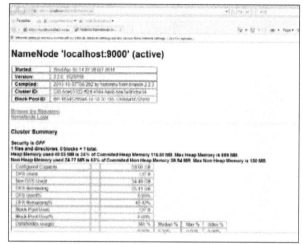

Figure 5: Working Node Manager

The output should be something like the message above along with: "*\hadoop\data\dfs\namenode has been successfully formatted*"

Starting HDFS daemons

Start namenode and datanode on the localhost by running the following command prompt:

```
C:\hdp\sbin>start-dfs.cmd
```

Two command prompts named namenode and datanode will open (Figure 2).

Start MapReduce or Yarn with the following command prompt:

```
C:\hdp\sbin>start-yarn.cmd
Starting yarn daemon
```

Two command prompts will open, named yarn nodemanager and yarn resourcemanager,

Verifying the installation

If the entire configuration and installation is successful, then open Internet Explorer to run Resource Manager and Node Manager at *http://localhost:8042* and Namenode at *http://localhost:50070*.

What Hadoop is *not*!

Hadoop is not a replacement for a database or a SAN file system.

It is not a substitute for a database: Hadoop does not index files but, instead, it stores data in files. In order to search for something, we have to run a MapReduce job, which goes through all data. Hadoop is suitable in a scenario where the data is too vast to be handled by a database.

MapReduce is not always the best algorithm:

MapReduce is a simple functional programming operation and it can be applied, in parallel, to gigabytes or terabytes of data. For that parallelism, you need to have each MR operation independent from all the others.

For more information refer to the Apache Hadoop link in Reference [5]. END

References

[1] http://www.oracle.com/technetwork/java/javase/downloads/jdk7-downloads-1880260.html
[2] http://www.microsoft.com/en-in/download/details.aspx?id=8442
[3] http://cygwin.com/setup-x86_64.exe
[4] http://www.apache.org/dist/hadoop/core/hadoop-2.2.0/hadoop-2.2.0-src.tar.gz
[5] http://wiki.apache.org/hadoop/HadoopIsNot
[6] http://hadoop.apache.org/
[7] https://svn.apache.org/viewvc/hadoop/common/branches/branch-2/BUILDING.txt?view=markup
[8] https://wiki.apache.org/hadoop/Hadoop2OnWindows
[9] http://en.wikipedia.org/wiki/Apache_Hadoop

By: Vinay Patkar and Avinash Bendigeri

Avinash works as a software development engineer at Dell R&D Centre, Bengaluru. He is interested in the automation and system management domains.

Vinay works as a software development engineer at Dell India R&D Centre, Bengaluru and has close to two years' experience in automation, Windows Server OS, and is interested in virtualisation and cloud computing technologies.

Run Linux on Windows

One of the many reasons to run Linux on Windows would be to get the best of both worlds. There are several methods for running Linux on Windows. The authors recommend Linux Integration Services, which has been made available by Microsoft. Read on to learn how to use LIS.

R ecent releases from Microsoft—'Windows Server 2012 R2' and 'System Centre 2012 R2'—comes with the ability to effectively host Linux and associated open source applications, along with great management capabilities. Some of the improvements in Windows Server 2012 R2 include faster live migration, dynamic memory support that can be used depending on workload, as well as the capability to dynamically resize VHDs and VHDXs. On the other hand, System Centre provides a single interface for managing Windows, ESXi and Linux operating systems. Microsoft's new feature from Windows Server 2012 R2 and System Center 2012 R2 called Data Centre Abstraction Layer (DAL), based on CIM and WS-Man standards,

has common management abstracts for managing all the resources of a data centre (this includes the physical and virtual environments). To support DAL, Microsoft has contributed Open Management Infrastructure (OMI) along with other providers to effectively manage Linux. OMI is well known for its smaller disk footprint.

This article will tell you how to use Windows Server 2012 R2 Hyper-V and Windows Hyper-V Server 2012 R2, and why installing Linux Integration Services is a best practice while running Linux as a guest OS.

Different ways of running Linux on Windows

Linux can be run on Windows in the following ways.

Virtual machines: Virtual machines are some of the best ways of running any operating system. The advantages of a VM include better hardware utilisation, the ability to run multiple OSs and to install and run any application. On a Windows machine, one can install third party virtualisation software like Virtual Box, VMware Player or Windows Hyper-V. Note that one can't install multiple virtualisation software on the same system.

The dual boot option: The dual boot option allows more than one operating system to reside on a single computer. In a dual boot, the Windows OS is stored on one volume/disk and the Linux OS on another volume/disk (assuming it is rarely used). The best use case would be to test a new OS without switching to it completely. This method is not the recommended way of running Linux alongside Windows, as the latter facilitates only partition-specific installation or on a logical partition (within an extended partition). The Microsoft recommendation is to install Windows on a primary partition. In order to dual boot a Windows machine, please refer to the link *https:// help.ubuntu.com/community/Installation/FromUSBStick*

Live USB and live CDs: A live USB is a USB flash drive or USB external hard drive containing the full operating system. It is the preferred way of running Linux when compared to a live CD, as data contained in the booting device can be changed and additional data can be stored in the USB. Refer to the link *https://help.ubuntu. com/community/Installation/FromUSBStick* to boot from a live USB.

Install Ubuntu via Wubi: Windows-based Ubuntu Installer (Wubi) is a software installer for Ubuntu. Wubi creates a special file on your Windows partition and uses that file as your Ubuntu drive without the need for a separate partition. This means that you can install Ubuntu and use it without any partitioning, and you can uninstall Ubuntu from the Windows Control Panel when your job is complete. Follow the link *http://www.howtogeek.com/howto/9142/ easily-install-ubuntu-linux-with-windows-using-the-wubi-installer/* to install Ubuntu using Wubi.

Cygwin: Cygwin is a collection of tools that offer a Linux-like shell environment on Windows, but it's not a method of running a full Linux distro. Follow the link *http://x.cygwin.com/docs/ug/setup-cygwin-x-installing.html* for download and installation instructions for Cygwin.

Installing Hyper-V role on Windows: To install Hyper-V role on Windows, you first need to take the following steps.

Preparing the hardware: Before you get started with enabling Hyper-V on Windows, make sure virtualisation technology is enabled via *BIOS--->Processor Settings---> Virtualization technology.*

Preparing the platform: In our example, let's use Windows Server 2012 R2 Datacentre SKU on the host machine.

On Windows Server 2012 R2, go to 'Start', type *Powershell ISE*, and then type the following commands:

```
PS C:\Windows\system32> Import-Module ServerManager
PS C:\Windows\system32> Get-WindowsFeature
PS C:\Windows\system32> Install-WindowsFeature Hyper-V
-Restart
```

However, the best practice for running Linux on Windows is to use Linux Integration Services.

Linux Integration Services

Microsoft developers have built drivers for Linux OSs and have released them through a package called Linux Integration Services (LISs), which are synthetic drivers for the network and disk that enhance I/O and networking performance.

To ensure compliance with the Linux community, the drivers have been reviewed by community and forum members, and have been checked into the main Linux kernel code base. Linux distribution vendors can now pull the drivers from the main Linux kernel and incorporate them into their respective distributions.

Microsoft made LIS open source so that anyone can build from source and make changes to the code. The main Github page for Linux Integration Services is *https://github. com/LIS* and the latest LIS package is 3.5. The code *(https:// github.com/LIS/LIS3.5)* for this has been released under the GNU Public License v2.

For more information on supported guest OSs on Windows OSs, please refer to the link *http://technet. microsoft.com/en-US/library/dn531026.aspx*

The following are some of the new features of LIS being introduced with Windows Server 2012 R2:
- *Kdump/Kexec:* Just like physical machines running the Linux OS, Linux guests can also get crash dumps.
- *Dynamic memory:* Based on the Linux guest OS' needs, memory can be automatically increased or decreased.
- *Linux Synthetic Frame Buffer Drivers:* Provides enhanced graphics performance for Linux desktop users.

You can refer to the following link for a detailed LIS feature list from Microsoft's *Virtualization* blog *http:// blogs.technet.com/b/virtualization/archive/2013/07/24/ enabling-linux-support-on-windows-server-2012-r2-hyper-v.aspx*

The following example will show you how to install LIS 3.5 for RHEL 6.3 running on Windows Server 2012 R2.

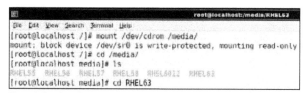

Figure 1: Run *install.sh* file

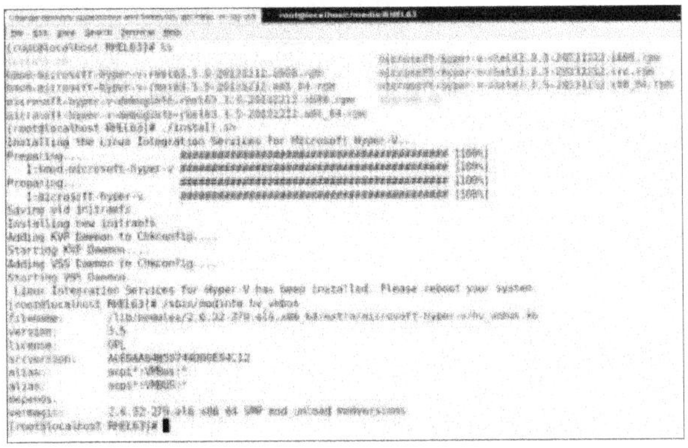

Figure 2: The LIS version for *hv_vmbus* after installing LIS 3.5

Installing Linux Integration Services (LIS)

- Create a Generation 1 virtual machine and install RHEL 6.3. Download LIS from *http://www.microsoft.com/en-us/download/details.aspx?id=41554*
- Connect to the virtual machine, and from the menu go to *Media ---> DVD Drive ---> Insert Disk* and attach LIS3.5 ISO.
- Open a terminal in the virtual machine running RHEL 6.3, and run the following commands as the root user to mount the ISO and navigate to the directory relevant distribution (in this case, it is RHEL 6.3):

```
[root@localhost ~]# mount /dev/cdrom /media/
[root@localhost ~]# cd /media/
```

- Locate the *install.sh* file, in our case */media/RHEL63/*, and run *install.sh* as shown in Figure 1. It should show the 'Install successful' message. To check whether LIS is installed properly, run the following commands from a terminal:

```
[root@localhost ~]# /sbin/modinfo hv_vmbus
[root@localhost ~]# /sbin/modinfo hv_netvsc
[root@localhost ~]# /sbin/modinfo hv_storvsc
[root@localhost ~]# /sbin/modinfo hv_blkvsc
[root@localhost ~]# /sbin/modinfo hv_util
```

Figure 2 shows the LIS version for '*hv_vmbus*' after installing LIS 3.5. END

References
- http://blogs.technet.com/b/virtualization/archive/2014/01/02/linux-integration-services-3-5-announcement.aspx

By: Vinay Patkar and Avinash Bendigeri

Vinay works as a software development engineer at Dell India R&D Centre, Bengaluru and has close to two years' experience in automation, Windows Server OS and is interested in virtualisation and cloud computing technologies.

Avinash works as a software development engineer at Dell R&D Centre, Bengaluru. He is interested in the automation and system management domains.

OSFY Magazine Attractions During 2014-15			
MONTH	THEME	FEATURED LIST	BUYERS GUIDE
March 2014	Network monitoring	Security	--------------------
April 2014	Android Special	Anti Virus	Wifi Hotspot devices
May 2014	Backup and Data Storage	Certification	External Storage
June 2014	Open Source on Windows	Mobile Apps	UTMs fo SME
July 2014	Firewall and Network security	Web hosting Solutions Providers	MFD Printers for SMEs
August 2014	Kernel Development	Big Data Solution Providers	SSD for servers
September 2014	Open Source for Start-ups	Cloud	Android devices
October 2014	Mobile App Development	Training on Programming Languages	Projectors
November 2014	Cloud special	Virtualisation Solutions Provider	Network Switches and Routers
December 2014	Web Development	A list of leading Ecommerce sites	AV Conferencing
January 2015	Programming Languages	IT Consultancy	Laser Printers for SMEs
February 2015	Top 10 of Everything on Open Source	Storage Solution Providers	Wireless routers

Configure Glassfish
on a Clustered Environment

Discover how to install and configure the Glassfish application server clustered environment on Red Hat Enterprise Linux Server 6.1.

G lassfish is a free and open source application server rolled out by Sun Microsystems for the Java EE platform, and is now sponsored by the Oracle Corporation. Using Glassfish, one can create enterprise applications that are both portable and scalable. This article continues from where the earlier write-up 'An Introduction to Glassfish: The Enterprise Application Server' left off.

Before proceeding with the installation, let us ensure that we are equipped with the following prerequisites:

1. Two servers are prepared with OS RHEL6.1. The hostname and IP address used are:
   First node   GF-Node01   192.168.10.10
   Second node   GF-Node02   192.168.10.11
2. Each server's '/etc/hosts' configuration file should contain the details of both the servers. It should look as shown below:

```
#cat /etc/hosts

127.0.0.1 localhost localhost.localdomain localhost4
localhost4.localdomain4
::1   localhost localhost.localdomain localhost6 localhost6.
localdomain6
192.168.10.10  GF-Node01.rsys.org      GF-Node01
192.168.10.11  GF-Node02.rsys.org      GF-Node02
```

3. Set the IP address as follows:
   [System -> Preferences -> Network Connection]

4. Turn off the firewall as follows:
   [System -> Administration -> Firewall]
5. SElinux setting can stay in its default Enforcing mode
   [Command to verify – getenforce; SElinux Configuration File – /etc/sysconfig/selinux]
6. Installation of Java: [jdk-1_5_0_20-linux-i586.rpm]
7. Glassfish application: [glassfish-installer-v2.1.1-b31g-linux.jar]
   Installations of Java and Glassfish have been covered in my previous article. So, without wasting any time let's proceed. Here, Glassfish is installed in /appinstall/glassfish.

Re-installing Glassfish Application Server

In case you want to re-install Glassfish, delete the 'glassfish' directory from where it is installed [in our case /appinstall/glassfish]. The reference command is # rm –rf /appinstall/glassfish

Browse to the directory in which you want to install Glassfish and then execute the following command:

```
# java -Xmx256m -jar /opt/Setup/glassfish-installer-v2.1.1-b31g-
linux.jar
```

 Note: The Glassfish setup is kept in '/opt/Setup'

Building a cluster over a standalone Glassfish application server

There may be a situation in which you already have Glassfish installed and built as a standalone application server. In such a scenario, DO NOT uninstall, but follow the procedure below which will help you to build Glassfish as a cluster over the standalone build.

Consider this to be the First Node:

GF-Node01   192.168.10.10

The added directories under */appinstall/glassfish*, after building a standalone application server are:

- bin
- config
- domains

Delete the above mentioned directories. The reference command is *# rm –rf bin/ config/ domains/*

Set *Executable Permission* to *'lib/ant/bin'* modules under the *'glassfish'* directory.

The reference command is *# chmod -R +x lib/ant/bin/* . Ideally, it will be set since the server was previously built as a standalone application server.

Using the 'ant' executable (located under */appinstall/ glassfish/lib/ant/bin)*, run *setup-cluster.xml*   (located under */ appinstall/glassfish)* to build a Glassfish cluster.

The reference command is *# lib/ant/bin/ant -f setup-cluster.xml*

As mentioned in my last article, under the Glassfish directory, there are two Glassfish *setup xml* files:

a. *setup.xml:* For building a standalone Glassfish environment.
b. *setup-cluster.xml:* For building a clustered Glassfish environment.

We know the build has been successful when we see the message *'BUILD SUCCESSFUL Total time: XX seconds'* followed by a return of the root prompt.

Note down the following port numbers which will be required later:

Admin Console	4848
HTTP Instance	8080
JMS	7676
IIOP	3700
HTTP_SSL	8181
IIOP_SSL	3820
IIOP_MUTUALAUTH	3920
JMX_ADMIN	8686

As observed, the deleted directories, *bin/, config/* and *domains/*, are recreated after a successful build. Verify if the build Glassfish application server supports clusters.

The reference command is:

```
# cd /appinstall/glassfish/bin
# ./asadmin
```

The build Glassfish application server supports clusters if the default domain 'domain1' starts successfully with the following message:

```
asadmin> start-domain
....::
```

```
Domain supports application server clusters and other
standalone instances.
asadmin>
```

> **Note:** The default credentials for 'Glassfish Administrative Console'are:
> Username   admin
> Password   adminadmin

Cluster configuration on GF-NODE 01

Before proceeding, just ensure that the domain is running.

There are three major components in creating a cluster:

- Creating a 'node agent' for both nodes.
- Creating a 'cluster' that will be common for both nodes - 'GF-Node01' and 'GF-Node02'.
- Creating 'instances' for both nodes.

Create the node agent 'GF-Agent01' for the first node 'GF-Node01' as follows:

```
asadmin> create-node-agent --host GF-Node01 --port 4848 GF-
Agent01
Please enter the admin user name>admin
Please enter the admin password>adminadmin
Command create-node-agent executed successfully.
asadmin>
```

Create the cluster 'GF-Cluster' that's common for both nodes 'GF-Node01' and 'GF-Node02' as follows:

```
asadmin> create-cluster --host GF-Node01 --port 4848 GF-Cluster
Please enter the admin user name>admin
Please enter the admin password>adminadmin
Command create-cluster executed successfully.
asadmin>
```

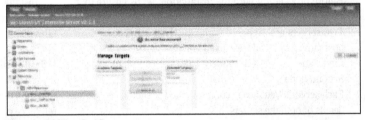

Figure 1: JDBCTimerPool-Error

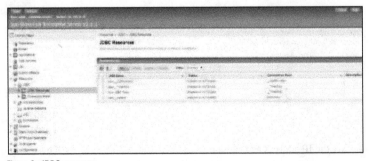

Figure 2: JDBC resources

Now create the instance 'GF-Instance01' for the first node 'GF-Node01':

```
asadmin> create-instance --host GF-Node01 --port
4848 --nodeagent GF-Agent01 --cluster GF-Cluster
GF-Instance01
Please enter the admin user name>admin
Please enter the admin password>adminadmin
Command create-instance executed successfully.
asadmin>
```

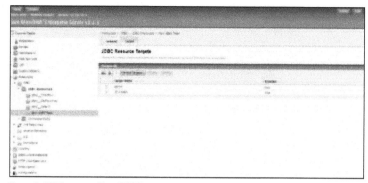

Figure 3: JDBC resource NewJDBCTimer

Start the node agent and instances for the first node 'GF-Node01':

```
asadmin> start-node-agent --syncinstances=true GF-Agent01

Please enter the admin user name>admin
Please enter the admin password>adminadmin
Please enter the master password [Enter to accept the default]:>
Redirecting output to /appinstall/glassfish/nodeagents/GF-
Agent01/agent/logs/server.log
Redirecting application output to /appinstall/glassfish/
nodeagents/GF-Agent01/agent/logs/server.log
Redirecting output to /appinstall/glassfish/nodeagents/GF-
Agent01/GF-Instance01/logs/server.log
Command start-node-agent executed successfully.

asadmin>
```

Making changes in JDBC resources

Now log in to the Glassfish administrative console
http://GF-Node01:4848 or *http://192.168.10.10:4848*

The hostname works if DNS is configured in your environment or the host file is configured on both the server and the client.

Browse to *Resources -> JDBC -> JDBC Resources ->
jdbc/__TimerPool*

On the right hand side, click on the 'Manage Target' tab.

Add 'GF-Cluster' (the cluster created above) from 'Available Targets' to 'Selected Targets'. On clicking 'OK', we encounter the error that is indicated in Figure 1.

In order to resolve the issue, create a new JDBC resource with the following details:

JNDI Name   New JDBC timer [this name can be
                anything of your choice]
Pool Name   _TimerPool [select from the drop-
                down menu]
Status   Enabled

Add 'GF-Cluster' from 'Available Targets' to 'Selected Targets'.

The JDBC resource 'New JDBC Timer' has been created successfully.

Browse to *Resources -> JDBC -> JDBC Resources-> New
JDBC Timer* and click on the *'Target'* tab. The 'GFCluster' should

be added and enabled. Refer to Figure 2 and Figure 3.

Next, browse to *Resources -> JDBC -> JDBC
Resources-> jdbc/__CallFlowPool* . 'GF-Cluster' should already be added and enabled under the 'Target' tab. Refer to Figure 4.

Now browse to *Resources -> JDBC -> JDBC Resources
-> jdbc/__default*.

Under the 'Target' tab, add the cluster 'GF-Cluster' from 'Available Targets' to 'Selected Targets'. As observed, the added cluster 'GF-Cluster' was not enabled [False]; it is now enabled [True]. Refer to Figure 5.

Once all the changes have been made under JDBC resources, we need to restart 'Nodeagent', 'Instance' and 'domain'.

```
#cd /appinstall/glassfish/bin
#./asadmin
```

Stop the node agent and instance on the first node 'GFNode01' as follows:

```
asadmin> stop-node-agent --stopinstances=true GF-Agent01
Command stop-node-agent executed successfully.
asadmin>
```

Stop the domain on the first node 'GF-Node01' as follows:

```
asadmin> stop-domain
Domain domain1 stopped.
asadmin>
```

Start the domain on the first node 'GF-Node01'as follows:

```
asadmin> start-domain
............
............


Domain supports application server clusters and other
standalone instances.

asadmin>
```

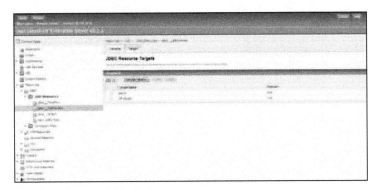

Figure 4: JDBC resource CallFlowPool

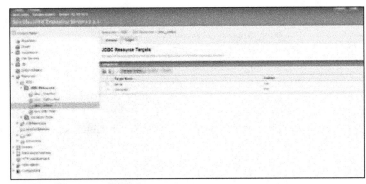

Figure 5: JDBC resource default

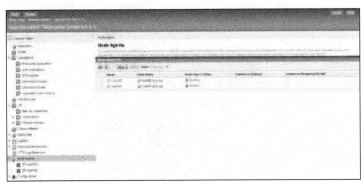

Figure 6: Node agents

Start the node agent and instance on the first node 'GF-Node01' as follows:

```
asadmin> start-node-agent --syncinstances=true GF-Agent01

Please enter the admin user name>admin
Please enter the admin password>adminadmin
Please enter the master password [Enter to accept the
default]:>
Redirecting output to /appinstall/glassfish/nodeagents/GF-
Agent01/agent/logs/server.log
Redirecting application output to /appinstall/glassfish/
nodeagents/GF-Agent01/agent/logs/server.log
Redirecting output to /appinstall/glassfish/nodeagents/GF-
Agent01/GF-Instance01/logs/server.log
```

```
Command start-node-agent executed successfully.

asadmin>
```

The cluster configuration on GF-Node02 is as follows:

Hostname	GF-Node02
GF-Node02	192.168.10.11

To summarise, you need to take the following steps:

1. Follow the pre-requisites section
2. Install Java: 'jdk-1_5_0_20-linux-i586.rpm'
3. Install Glassfish: 'glassfish-installer-v2.1.1-b31g-linux.jar'
4. Set the recursive executable permission to the *'lib/ant/bin'* directory under 'glassfish'.
The reference command is: *# chmod -R +x lib/ant/bin/*
5. Build Glassfish to support the application cluster.
The reference command is: *# lib/ant/bin/ant -f setup-cluster.xml*

Once completed, DO NOT start the default domain 'domain1' on this Node 'GF-Node02'; check with the reference command given below:

```
#cd /appinstall/glassfish/bin
#./asadmin

asadmin>stop-domain
The domain (domain1) isn't running.
asadmin>
```

Create the node agent 'GF-Agent02' on the second node 'GF-Node02' referring to the first node 'GF-Node01', as follows:

```
asadmin>create-node-agent --host GF-Node01 --port
4848 GF-Agent02

Please enter the admin user name>admin
Please enter the admin password>adminadmin
Command create-node-agent executed successfully.

asadmin>
```

Create the instance 'GF-Instance02' on the second node 'GF-Node02' referring to the first node 'GF-Node01', as follows:

```
asadmin>create-instance --host GF-Node01 --port 4848
--nodeagent GF-Agent02 --cluster GF-Cluster GF-Instance02

Please enter the admin user name>admin
Please enter the admin password>adminadmin
Command create-instance executed successfully.

asadmin>
```

Figure 7: Cluster

Figure 8: Web application deployed

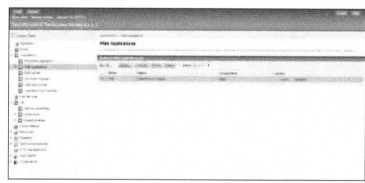

Figure 9: Undeploy

Now start the node agent and instances for the second node 'GF-Node02':

```
asadmin> start-node-agent --syncinstances=true GF-Agent02

Please enter the admin user name>admin
Please enter the admin password>adminadmin
Please enter the master password [Enter to accept the
default]:>
Redirecting output to /appinstall/glassfish/nodeagents/GF-
Agent02/agent/logs/server.log
Redirecting application output to /appinstall/glassfish/
nodeagents/GF-Agent02/agent/logs/server.log
Redirecting output to /appinstall/glassfish/nodeagents/GF-
Agent02/GF-Instance02/logs/server.log
Command start-node-agent executed successfully.
```

```
asadmin>
```

> **Note:**
> a. While creating a node agent and an instance on the second node 'GF-Node02', the cluster mentioned is 'GF-Cluster' which was earlier created in 'GF-Node01'.
> b. The admin user name and password used above are that of the first node 'GF-Node01.

Verifying the cluster configuration

Login to admin console - *http://<IP Address or FQDN>:4848*

> **Note:** Turn off the firewall of the Linux server or allow the required port numbers, without which the admin console will not be accessible. Both node agents and the cluster is up and running (see Figure 6 and Figure 7).

Deploying a sample Web application on a clustered environment

Download a sample WAR file to test. In our case, it is 'hello.war'. Log in to the Glassfish admin console. Go to *Application -> Web Applications*. Click on *Deploy*. Keeping the default selection, choose the file *'hello.war'*. Add 'GF-Cluster' from 'Available Targets' to 'Selected Targets'. Click 'OK'.

The Web application 'hello.war' has now been deployed successfully (Figure 8).

Click on 'Launch' under 'Action'. The links given below will be displayed for the 'hello' application:

- *http://GF-Node01.rsys.org:8080/hello*
- *https://GF-Node01.rsys.org:8181/hello*
- *http://gf-node01.rsys.org:38080/hello*
- *https://gf-node01.rsys.org:38181/hello*
- *http://gf-node02.rsys.org:38080/hello*
- *https://gf-node02.rsys.org:38181/hello*

As observed, the Web application deployed from the admin console of 'GF-Node01' can be accessible from both the nodes ('GF-Node01' and 'GF-Node02').

How to 'undeploy' a Web application on a clustered environment

Under *Application -> Web Application*, check the WAR file. The 'Undeploy' button will be enabled (Figure 9), so click on it. The Web Application undeploys successfully. END

By: Arindam Mitra

The author is an assistant manager in a Pune-based IT company. Contact him at *mail2arindam2003@yahoo.com* or *arindam0310018@gmail.com*

Asia's #1 Conference
on Open Source

11th Edition

OPEN
SOURCE INDIA
NIMHANS Convention Center

7 - 8
November
2014

BENGALURU

**FREEZE Your
Calendar NOW!**

NOVEMBER
7-8 2014

For more details, call Omar (+91-9958881862) or email us at **info@osidays.com**

Organisers

 EFYGROUP

Media Partners

  EFYtimes.com electronics OpenSourceForYou

Simplify Life with
VirtualBox

VirtualBox allows you to run a number of instances of operating systems on a single machine and seamlessly switch from one OS to another. This article covers how a VirtualBox may be set up on a Windows machine and how it can be used to run other OSs like Windows 8.1 and Chromium. Other uses of VirtualBox are also featured.

VirtualBox has been around for seven years now and it is a good free and open source alternative to proprietary virtualisation platforms like VMware, Microsoft Hyper –V, etc. It provides all the functionality that one expects from a virtualisation platform, and with Oracle as its backbone one need not worry about quality and support.

In this article, we'll tackle some challenges and work out solutions using VirtualBox. However, if you wish to first familiarise yourself with virtualisation concepts and terminology, please refer to the article titled 'Kick-Starting Virtualisation with VirtualBox' published in the March 2013 edition of *Open Source For You*.

Downloading and installing VirtualBox

Follow these steps to download and install VirtualBox on your machine.

Step 1: Navigate to *https://www.virtualbox.org/wiki/Downloads* and download the VirtualBox setup file for Microsoft Windows. The current version, at the time of writing this article, is 4.3.10.

Step 2: Open the location where the setup file has been downloaded and execute the file named *VirtualBox-4.3.10-93012-Win.exe*.

Step 3: Proceed with the installation in the following manner.
Welcome **window:** Press *Next*.
Custom Setup **window:** Change installation location if you wish to install VirtualBox in a different location, or else leave everything as is and press *Next*. Uncheck the default settings if you do not wish VirtualBox icons to appear on the desktop or the *Quick Launch* bar. However, keep the *Register file associations* box checked (this will ensure that files associated with VirtualBox open only with VirtualBox). Then press *Next*.
Network Interfaces Warning **window:** During installation, VirtualBox will reset the network connections. So make sure that any network dependent tasks are completed before proceeding. Press *Yes* when ready.
Ready to Install **window:** Press *Install* to begin the installation.

> **Note:** VirtualBox needs to install a few drivers in order to complete the installation. Check *Always trust software from "Oracle Corporation"* and press *Install* when the pop-up is displayed.

Installation Complete **window:** It should take about 5-6 minutes for the installation to complete. Keep the *'Start Oracle VirtualBox 4.3.10 after installation'* option checked and press *Finish*.

Use-case 1: Create a remote PC and remote storage

Amidst all the chaos around governments breaching our privacy and cloud storage vendors' data centres getting hacked, one thought that often crosses one's mind is: "If only I had my own cloud storage." Look no further. With VirtualBox, a virtual machine (VM) can be created and remote access can be allowed to it. This will eliminate the risk of the host system getting exposed and will provide a sandboxed environment for accessing data remotely. This VM can also be used as a remote PC for working on the go.

Creating the VM

We'll be using Microsoft Windows 8.1 Enterprise. A 90-day evaluation version of Windows 8.1 Enterprise can be downloaded from *http://goo.gl/P7E0q5*.

> **Note:** A Microsoft account is required to download this image file. In case you don't have a Microsoft account, create one at *http://goo.gl/JDNIZZ*.

Once the image file has finished downloading, open VirtualBox and follow the instructions given below to create the VM.

Step 1: In the VirtualBox console, press the *New* icon and fill in the information, as shown in Figure 1, in the *Name* and *Operating system* window before pressing *Next*.

> **Note:** In the above window, the *Windows 8.1 (64-bit)* option has been selected. 64-bit options will appear only if the host system has a 64-bit processor and it supports virtualisation technology. By default, most systems have the virtualisation support option disabled, so you'll need to enable it in the BIOS.

> **Note:** If you are using the 32-bit image of Windows 8.1, select the Windows 8.1 (32-bit) option from the Version drop-down list.

Step 2: By default, VirtualBox assigns 2048 MB of RAM to a Windows 8.1 virtual machine. You can increase it to any amount as long as the pointer lies in the green area (as shown in Figure 2). Press *Next*, once done.

> **Note:** 2048 MB of RAM is recommended only if you're not planning to run any memory intensive applications (e.g., Microsoft Office, an antivirus, etc) on the VM. If you wish to use this VM as an alternate PC, you may want to increase the RAM to a more suitable amount.

Steps 3 - 5: In the next three windows, select the following options:
- Hard drive: *Create a virtual hard drive now*
- Hard drive file type: *VDI (VirtualBox Disk Image)*
- Storage on physical hard drive: *Dynamically allocated*

Step 6: Specify the location and size of the virtual hard drive. Though 25 GB, available by default, will be sufficient for the purposes of this article, you can set it to any amount, depending on the free storage capacity available on the host system. Once done, press *Create*.

Step 7: Before switching on the VM, we'll need to point it to the *Windows 8.1 Enterprise* (90-day evaluation) image file to install the operating system. To do this select *Windows 8.1* and press the *Settings* icon in the top menu. Select *Storage* and then select *Empty* under the *Controller: IDE* section. Press the disk icon in the *Attributes* section, and select the *Choose a virtual CD/ DVD disk file* option. Navigate to the location of the image file, select it and press *Open*. Press *OK* to close the *Settings* window.

Step 8: Press *Start* in the top menu and proceed with the Windows 8.1 installation.

> **Note:** Post installation, select *Use Express Settings* on the *Settings* page.

Step 9: The last step in this section is to install *VirtualBox Guest Additions* on the virtual machine. To do this, select the *Insert Guest Additions CD Image* option from the *Devices* menu in the *Virtual Machine* window. Open *This*

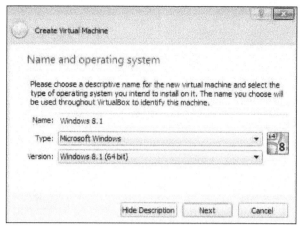

Figure 1: Name and operating system window

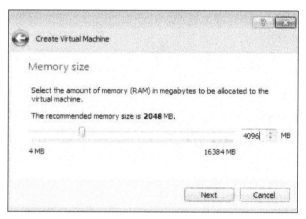

Figure 2: Allocate memory size

PC on the VM, double click on *VirtualBox Guest Additions CD Drive* and proceed with the installation. Reboot the VM when the installation is finished.

Setting up shared folders

Once the virtual machine is ready, we'll need to set up a shared folder between the host system and the VM. This folder will be used to place the files you want to access remotely.

To set up a shared folder, follow these instructions. In the VirtualBox console, select *Windows 8.1*. Click on the *Settings* icon and select *Shared Folders*. Press the + icon to add a folder and specify the desired folder path. Specify the folder name, as it should appear in the VM (without spaces). Uncheck *Read-only*. Check *Auto-mount*, press *OK* and close the *Settings* window.

Start the VM and open *This PC*. The shared folder should appear as a drive, as shown in Figure 6.

Accessing the shared folder remotely

Now that our backend setup is in place, let's work to make it remotely accessible. We'll do this with the help of Teamviewer, which is a must-have remote desktop sharing tool. In addition to its core functionality, it provides features like remote file sharing, virtual meetings, etc. Also, since it

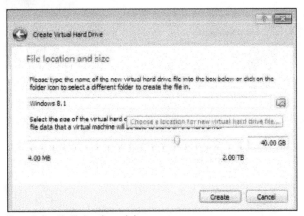

Figure 3: Specify file location and size

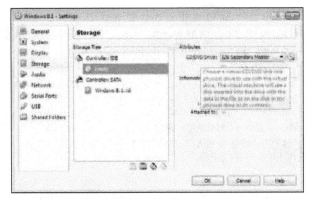

Figure 4: Mount the installation image file

has a mobile client for all major platforms, it ensures that you will have access to your data irrespective of the type of device you use.

Log on to *http://www.teamviewer.com* from the VM, download the setup and install it.

> **Note:** If you do not wish to install Teamviewer, there is an option to execute it in *Run-only (One time use)* mode. Also, in response to *'How do you wish to use it?'*, select *Personal / non-commercial* as we're using it for personal use only.

Once Teamviewer is up and running, note down the ID and password shown under the *Allow Remote Control* section. These credentials will be used to access this VM remotely.

Next, on your mobile device (we'll use an Android device for the purpose of this article) install the Teamviewer app from the Google Play store (or the respective app store for your device). Open the app and follow the instructions displayed on the screens as shown in Figure 7.

You can also install productivity applications (like Adobe Reader, Office 365, etc) on the Windows 8.1 VM and convert it into an on-the-fly office. Some sample screens of this VM, when accessed via an Apple iPad, are shown in Figure 8.

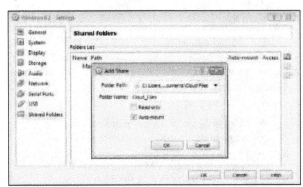

Figure 5: Specify shared folder details

Figure 6: Cloud files shared folder in the VM

Use-case 2: Try Chrome OS with VirtualBox

Google Chromebook is the latest offering in the world of thin client computing. While you can buy a Chromebook for around Rs 22,000, you can own a virtual one for free. To know how, keep reading.

Chromebook runs on Chrome OS, which is the commercial version of Chromium OS (a Linux-based open source project initiated by Google). So all that needs to be done is to download the VirtualBox image of Chromium OS and create a VM to run it.

Downloading Chromium OS

Navigate to *http://goo.gl/pXLro* and download the VirtualBox

image of Chromium OS compiled by Hexxeh.

Once the download is complete, extract the zipped file to a folder named *Chromium OS*. Next, we'll need to create a VM for this image to run.

Creating a VM from a VirtualBox image

Open VirtualBox and create a new VM based on the following instructions:

- Name and operating system
  - Name: Chromium OS
  - Type: Linux
  - Version: Other Linux (32-bit)
- Memory size: 1024 MB

Note: It can also work with 512 MB of RAM but that's recommended only when the host machine has 2 GB, or less, of RAM.

- Hard drive: Select the *Use an existing virtual hard drive file* option and spe Use an existing virtual hard drive file cify the location of the extracted Chromium OS VDI file and press *Create*.
- Settings configuration: Before starting the Chromium OS VM, the following settings need to be in place:

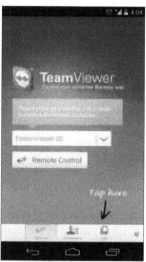

Figure 7: Accessing the shared folder on an Android device

  - Enable *Physical Address Extension:* Navigate to *Settings > System > Processor* and check *Enable PAE/NX*
  - Network adapter type: Navigate to *Settings > Network > Adapter 1 > Advanced* and change the adapter type to *Intel PRO/1000 MT Desktop (82540EM)*

Executing the VM

In the VirtualBox console, select *Chromium OS* and press *Start* from the top menu.

On starting, the VM window will show the notifications regarding *Auto capture keyboard* and *Mouse Pointer Integration* stating that the VM supports these features and they have been turned on by default.

For some reason, the mouse integration doesn't work well with *Chromium OS* VM, so we'll need to disable it for the mouse pointer to work in the VM environment. Do so by selecting *Disable Mouse Pointer Integration* from the *Machine* menu in the VM window. The next time you click inside the VM window, the pop-up shown in Figure 9 will appear.

Check *Do not show this message again* and press *Capture*.

Chromium OS

On the first run, Chromium OS will require you to specify certain settings for it to work. Once the configuration is complete, you'll be shown the welcome screen.

Congratulations! You're now the proud owner of a virtual Chromebook. To explore more, visit the official *Chromebook Help* website at *http://goo.gl/Lz2aBC*.

Apart from running other OSs, there are several uses to which a VirtualBox can be put.

Use-case 3: Run legacy applications and operating systems

In the course of a day's work, one may come across applications which will only run on a particular configuration.

Figure 8: Accessing the VM on an Apple iPad

For example, even today, there are many Web-based applications that can only run on Internet Explorer 6. These configurations might be obsolete (just like IE 6) and can be hard to find in a production environment.

Apart from these, there could be times when a vendor stops supporting a version of an operating system, and since organisations cannot make a switch easily, they will be stuck. One recent example is Microsoft withdrawing support for Windows XP.

In situations like these, VirtualBox can be of great help. Create a VM of that particular configuration or operating system and move on with life. These VMs can be used till the applications are ported to a newer configuration or OS, and then can be discarded.

Use-case 4: Test suspicious files

Let's assume that you've got an email from a friend that has an attachment, but you're feeling a bit sceptical about it. Why take a risk by opening it on your system? Use VirtualBox. Create a master VM, clone it and open the attachment on the clone. Once you're sure about the integrity of the file, discard the clone. This setup can also come in handy if you like to study or experiment with computer viruses. You can unleash the virus on one of the clones and then study its effect on it —all the fun without compromising the security of the host system.

Use-case 5: Set up a multi-platform development environment

VirtualBox can be a real boon for application and Web developers. Using VirtualBox, they can set up a development environment comprising various platforms (servers, Windows, Linux, Solaris, etc) and with the help of the shared folders feature, a central repository of code can be set up. This code can then be tested on different platforms. This saves you the trouble of setting up a physical lab and then replicating code on each of the systems.

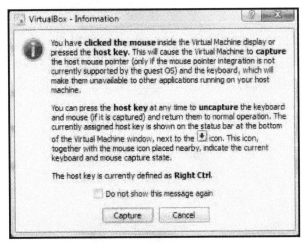

Figure 9: VirtualBox mouse capture notification

Use-case 6: Create a virtual lab to learn enterprise software

This is by far one of my favourite use cases of VirtualBox. Being a curious Tom, I love to get my hands dirty by learning the enterprise software used at work—mail server software, directory software, whatever. VirtualBox is a wonderful resource in such cases. You can use it to create a mini-virtual lab consisting of server(s) and a few client machines. You can then deploy the software you wish to learn in this virtual lab and experiment with it.

Best practices and recommendations

A few tips and tricks can go a long way to help you get the best out of VirtualBox. Based on my experience with it, I am listing a few below.

Use a 64-bit processor: Usually, a machine with a 32-bit processor limits the usable RAM to 3 GB. This, in turn, limits the amount of RAM you can assign to a VM and also the number of VMs you can create. On the other hand, a 64-bit processor gives you the flexibility to use up to 16 GB of RAM on the host system, thereby increasing the amount of RAM that can be allocated to VMs.

Enable virtualisation in the BIOS: As stated earlier, most of the systems have this feature disabled, by default. If you wish to create 64-bit VMs, you'll need to enable this option in the BIOS.

Use NAT: Unless you're planning to create an internal network, use NAT as a network mode. This would save you the trouble of configuring the VM to access the Internet, because with NAT VMs hide behind the IP address of the host machine and can access the Internet as long as host system has access to it.

Use auto-mount for shared folders: Keeping the auto-mount setting checked while creating the shared folder will ensure that the folder is visible as soon as the VM boots up.

Use a separate partition or hard drive: By default, VirtualBox stores the VM files in the C drive. This can fill the drive pretty fast, if you're working with multiple VMs. In order to keep the C drive clean, it is recommended that you use either a separate partition or a hard drive to store the VMs.

Install guest additions: VirtualBox guest additions install certain drivers on the VM, which enable it to function like a normal machine. For example, without guest additions installed, a VM will not occupy the full screen even in the *Full Screen* mode.

RAM allocation: Never allocate more than 75 per cent of available RAM to a single VM or else the host system's performance will be affected. You must keep RAM allocation within the green region in the *Memory Size* window.

Common errors and resolutions

Error: VT-x/AMD-V hardware acceleration has been enabled, but is not operational

This error comes up when you're trying to boot a 64-bit VM but VirtualBox isn't able to find hardware virtualisation capabilities on the host machine. This can be fixed by turning on the VT - x or *Virtualization* option in the BIOS.

Error: 0x0000225

This error is related to I/O APIC (Advanced Programmable Interrupt Controllers) settings. APIC provides a mechanism by which the devices attached to the VM communicate with the processor. If you're using a 64-bit VM, I/O APIC settings need to be enabled. You can enable this by going to *Settings > System* and checking 'Enable I/O APIC' in the *Extended Features* section.

Error: Error loading operating system

This is the most common type of error that users face when migrating Windows VMs from VMware to VirtualBox. This can be fixed easily by changing the controller of the virtual hard drive from SCSI to IDE and then repairing the boot manager using the installation disk. The link *http://goo.gl/PzOAyo* contains a detailed tutorial on fixing this error.

Besides the above mentioned use cases, virtualisation technology also makes it possible to optimally use hardware. Organisations are today implementing a virtualised infrastructure for their employees to work in. This not only reduces the amount of e-waste but also serves as a secure computing environment. Even home users can efficiently utilise their old hardware with the help of virtualisation tools like VirtualBox.

If you have any other use case for VirtualBox, or if you use VirtualBox to tackle any other day-to-day challenges, do share them. END

By: Uday Mittal

The author is an open source enthusiast who likes to experiment with new technologies. He works in the field of information security and can be reached at *mailme@udaymittal.com*.

Accessing Linux Data Partitions
from Windows

In a dual boot Windows-Linux computer, it is comparatively easier to view the
Windows partitions from Linux, than the other way round, i.e., viewing Linux partitions
from Windows. In this article, the author presents a way around this challenge.

Today, in the world of computers, dual booting or running both Windows and Linux on the same system, is fairly common. In which case, users often want to transfer files/data between the two operating systems. Linux has native support for Windows file systems (NTFS and FAT), which means that you can access Windows partitions from Linux. But, this is not the case with Windows. To access Linux partitions from Windows, you need third-party software, specifically designed for this purpose.

Basic differences between Windows and Linux file systems

The file systems used in Windows and Linux are completely different in many ways – from how the disks and devices are enumerated to the level of data security provided by them. The file systems used in Windows are FAT (FAT12, FAT16 and FAT32) and NTFS – this last variant is the most used file system in all new Windows operating systems. Linux supports a greater number of file systems like Ext2, Ext3, Ext4, XFS, JFS, etc. The predominant file system used in Linux is Ext3.

On Windows, a disk is divided into partitions and exposed to the user through a drive letter. Even the CD-ROM and removable media get a drive letter. Linux doesn't use drive letters. On Linux, everything is under the root directory (/). Linux treats all the devices as files. All devices like disks and CD-ROMs connected to Linux will be mounted to the root directory or to any other directory under the root like /dev/sda and /dev/cdrom, respectively.

The Windows file system is not case sensitive but Linux file systems are. For example, you can't have file names like mickey.txt and Mickey.txt in the same directory in Windows. In Linux however, file names like mickey.txt and Mickey.txt can reside in the same directory.

On Windows, the application locks exclusive access to files, whereas Linux doesn't lock exclusive access to the file as often as Windows does. For example, after watching a video file in VLC on Windows, if you try to delete it without closing the VLC player or opening another file in it—you'll see an error message. You need to stop watching the file in VLC before you can delete it, rename it, or do anything else to it. But Linux allows you to delete the file once it is closed from the VLC player.

Tools used to access the Linux partition from Windows

There are various open source tools available on the Web that you can use to access the Linux partitions from a Windows system. These are categorised based on their uses and functionality.
- Tools used to read and write on the Linux partition
- Tools used for 'read only' access to the Linux partition

Tools use to read and write on the Linux partition

Ext2Fsd*: This tool provides options to assign drive letters, to flush the cache to disk, to view advanced properties for a drive or partition, etc.

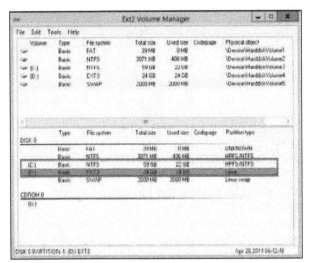

Figure 1: Ext2 volume manager

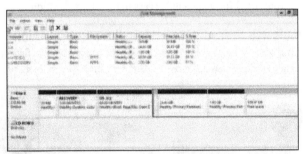

Figure 2: Ext2 IFS

Figure 3: Explore2fs

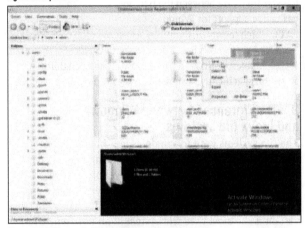

Figure 4: DiskInternals Linux reader

Figure 1 shows the Linux partition after assigning a drive letter. The 'Service Management' feature of Ext2Fsd will enable you to view the current status of Ext2Fsd service which need to start it manually. It also provides the option to set all volumes to be loaded in 'read-only' mode or read/write mode. Ext2Fsd provides limited Ext4 support and by default, it will load the file systems in read-only mode.

Ext2 IFS* (Installable File System): Ext2 IFS provides Windows with full access to Linux Ext2/Ext3 volumes. It installs a pure kernel mode file system driver, Ext2fs.sys, which actually extends the Windows operating system to include the Ext2 file system. You can view the Linux partition listed in the disk management as shown in Figure 2. This tool also adds the 'IFS drives' item to the control panel from where you can assign a drive letter to Linux partitions.

*On Win8 onwards, Ext2 Volume manager and Ext2 IFS need to be run with *Compatibility mode* enabled.

Tools used for 'read only' access to the Linux partition

Explore2fs: This is a GUI explorer tool for accessing Ext2 and Ext3 file systems. It runs under all versions of Windows and can read almost any Ext2 and Ext3 file system. You can save the content on your Windows partitions to make any changes to the files as shown in Figure 3.

DiskInternals Linux reader: This runs under Windows and allows you to access *Ext2/Ext3/Ext4* Linux files. It provides read-only access to the Linux partition and does not allow you to make changes in file system partitions. Also, it uses Windows Explorer to view and extract files/data. Figure 4 shows its usage.

The tools listed are the ones that we have used and found very useful in dual boot scenarios. There are many more tools available on the Internet, which can be used for accessing Linux partitions from Windows, but they may not be compatible with the latest Windows OS. END

References

You can get the above-mentioned tools from the following locations:
[1] Ext2fsd: http://sourceforge.net/projects/ext2fsd/
[2] Ext2IFS: http://www.fs-driver.org/index.html
[3] Ext2read: http://sourceforge.net/projects/ext2read/
[4] Explore2fs: http://www.chrysocome.net/explore2fs

By: Perumalraja P and Abhijit Sune

Perumal works as a lead engineer in enterprise operating system group at Dell India R&D Centre, Bengaluru and has 10+ years of experience in Windows operating system and applications. His area of interest are deployment and storage related technologies.

Abhijit works as a Windows engineer in Dell India R&D Centre, Bengaluru and has 6+ years of experience in Windows operating system and applications. His area of interest are System Management and Deployment related technologies.

Run a WordPress-based Site on a Windows Server

Let's go through the process of installing and running a WordPress-based site on a Windows server.

WordPress is open source content management software that is very widely used across the world to create websites and blogs. One of the major advantages of WordPress is its plug and play architecture. Its versatility and millions of plugins allows you to customise your sites and gives you a competitive edge. Currently, there are many e-commerce and private social network sites that use WordPress.

WordPress can either be used online at *www.wordpress.com* or accessed as a downloadable version at *www.wordpress.org*.

Though it is open source software, it can be hosted either on an open source-based platform or on a Windows-based Web platform, in order to build custom sites. Microsoft provides a robust Web platform and a set of comprehensive tools which can be used to host WordPress. Microsoft's Web platform interface for hosting WordPress is the key focus of this article.

An introduction to Web Server Roles or IIS

The Microsoft Windows Server family provides numerous server roles that can handle complex IT tasks. One of the main roles used in configuring and managing Web-based applications is the Web Server Role or Internet Information Services (IIS). Windows' Web Server Role lets you share information with users on the Internet, an intranet, or extranet, using sites, pages, etc. Using this, you can deploy and manage websites and applications across large farms of Web servers from a central place. One of the major advantages of using IIS is its scalability and open architecture.

Windows Server 2008 and Windows Server 2008 R2 deliver IIS 7, which is a unified Web platform that integrates IIS, ASP. NET, Windows Communication Foundation and Windows SharePoint Services. Microsoft introduced IIS 8.5 with Windows Server 2012 R2, which has helped it improve support for organisations that have a large number of websites to manage.

Prerequisites for hosting WordPress on a Windows-based system

Before you install WordPress with Microsoft Web Platform, ensure that the following prerequisites are in place on your Windows system.

WordPress prerequisites: *http://wordpress.org/about/requirements/*

IIS prerequisites: *http://msdn.microsoft.com/en-us/library/cc268240.aspx*

Installing WordPress on a Windows-based system

Microsoft WebMatrix and Microsoft Web Platform Installer (Web PI) are two very effective tools from Microsoft that automate the installation of WordPress. With these tools, you have the option to install not only Microsoft-based Web components but also a huge set of open source applications and built-in templates. Both these tools can be used to successfully install and host WordPress on a Windows-based system in order to create, publish and maintain your websites. These tools install the latest components of the Microsoft Web Platform including Internet Information Services (IIS), SQL Server Express, .NET Framework and Visual Web Developer.

To host a site from a Windows-based system using WordPress, you will need to install one of the following tools and use it to download and install WordPress and all the other required applications. Given below are the basic guidelines for installing WordPress using these tools. Ensure that your system is connected to the Internet before starting the process. You can also download all the required components offline and install WordPress. Using an online method with these tools is recommended, as it always fetches the data dynamically and allows you to install the latest supported components.

Using Microsoft WebMatrix

1. Download and install Microsoft WebMatrix from *http://www.microsoft.com/web/gallery/install. aspx?appid=webmatrix* on your system. It will automatically install the other additional components like IIS and Microsoft SQL Server Express.
2. Once installed, you can just open Microsoft WebMatrix and click on 'Site from Web Gallery' to select WordPress for installation.

> **Note:** With WebMatrix 3, just after installation, you will have to select *New->App Gallery* to open the option 'Site from Web Gallery'.

3. As prerequisites, along with WordPress, it also downloads and installs MySQL and PHP packages automatically.
4. WordPress needs a database to be installed for data management. So you can create a new database using the MySQL database that was downloaded and installed.
5. During the process, you might have to set the credentials for accessing the database that will be used by WordPress.
6. Once the WordPress installation is complete, open the WebMatrix site workspace to launch your WordPress site by clicking on the 'Run' button. This page gives you the URL or permalink of your site.
7. Here you can also access the source PHP pages for your site from the files workspace. You can modify the pages as per your requirement and once you have modified them, you will have to click on 'Run again' from WebMatrix to launch your site.
8. Your site has now been launched using the default Web browser (e.g., Internet Explorer).
9. Now log in to your site using the required credentials and access the WordPress dashboard to modify your site. For detailed steps on how to use the WordPress dashboard, visit Reference 6 below.
   For a detailed step by step guide refer to *http://www. microsoft.com/web/post/your-first-website-using-webmatrix*.

Using Microsoft's Web Platform Installer (Web PI)

1. Download and install Microsoft's Web Platform Installer from *http://www.microsoft.com/web/downloads/platform. aspx* on your system.
2. Under the 'Applications' category in the Web PI, you can add a set of open source applications to install them in your system. Add 'WordPress' to install it on your system.
3. The Web PI also downloads and installs MySQL and PHP packages along with WordPress.
4. As mentioned above, you will need to create a new database that can be used by WordPress to store its contents.
5. Now you can open an Internet Explorer page and access your WordPress dashboard by opening your site as *http://localhost/<your site name>*.

6. At this page, provide the required information to complete the WordPress installation.
7. Now you can log in to your site using the required credentials and access the WordPress dashboard to modify your site. For detailed steps on using the WordPress dashboard, visit *http://codex.wordpress. org/Administration_Screens* (see References at the end of the article).
   For a detailed step by step guide, refer to *http://codex. wordpress.org/Installing_on_Microsoft_IIS*.
   Once you have created, modified and published your site using WordPress, it can be accessed using your system's hostname or IP address.

Tips and best practices

You can create either a self-hosted site or a free site at WordPress.com. While a self-hosted site may require some initial investment and maintenance costs, a free site may not be best suited for all your requirements as the URL for the site will be something like *yoursitename.wordpress. com*. So depending on the purpose of your site and your budget, make your choice.

Make a habit of updating your WordPress version, as well as your site, to avoid any security vulnerability. But make sure you have proper backup for your site. For WordPress backup options, refer to *http://codex. wordpress.org/WordPress_Backups*.

Windows Live writer is another free tool from Microsoft, which can be integrated with WordPress to easily modify your WordPress site's contents and to add pictures or videos. You can download it from *http://www.microsoft. com/en-in/download/details.aspx?id=8621*.

For a comprehensive list of WordPress best practices, do refer to *http://vip.wordpress.com/documentation/best-practices/*. END

References

[1] *http://codex.wordpress.org/First_Steps_With_WordPress*
[2] *http://codex.wordpress.org/Working_with_WordPress*
[3] *http://easywpguide.com/*
[4] *http://www.iis.net/*
[5] *http://www.microsoft.com/web/downloads/*
[6] *http://codex.wordpress.org/Administration_Screens*

By: Barun Chaudhary and Gobind Vijayakumar

Barun Chaudhary is a lead engineer in the Enterprise Operating System group at Dell India R&D Centre, Bengaluru. He has 7+ years of experience in the Windows operating system and on server virtualization technologies. His areas of interest cover virtualization and cloud computing technologies.

Gobind Vijayakumar works in the OS Engineering group at Dell India R&D Centre, Bengaluru, and has 5+ years of experience in Windows Server operating system and its applications. His interests include server, storage and networking technologies.

Get Your DokuWiki
Running on Windows!

A wiki is a Web application that allows one to modify, add, delete or edit content in collaboration with others. The most popular example of it would be Wikipedia. DokuWiki is simple to use, highly versatile open source wiki software which does not need a database. Read on to learn how to go about setting up a DokuWiki.

okuWiki is the most simple, flexible and extensible Wiki around. It can store content in a flat file, instead of a typical database. So, while your application runs on different devices, the data can be stored on the cloud, to be accessed from many different computing devices.

Key features

A wiki is a powerful Web authoring mechanism that simplifies content creation without the need for much knowledge of mark-up languages like HTML. There are many wikis around that you could run on a LAMP or a WAMP stack. DokuWiki has the features of a regular wiki, such as being able to create Web content, allow editing by multiple users, format documents and store media such as images or documents.

A special feature that stands out in DokuWiki is the plain text files that store content. Content stored as plain text files has several advantages. You do not need to run databases such as MySQL where you have hosted the wiki. This not only means

fewer overheads to set up and administer but also easy data backup and restore. Another advantage of having plain text files is that they can be stored on cloud services (like Google Drive or Dropbox). This makes your wiki content accessible across Windows PCs, Mac laptops or Ubuntu desktops. Also, since the content is in plain text, you can view the files in Notepad even on a mobile device.

Extensions are another key distinguishing feature of DokuWiki. They come as themes and also functional add-ons. Themes help in personalising the layout, the organisation of data and the look-and-feel, whereas add-ons (also known as plugins) extend the functionality of the wiki. There are already dozens of themes and hundreds of plugins to choose from. If you still need customisation, writing a plugin or theme is easy!

Setting up DokuWiki on Windows

To set up DokuWiki, you just need Apache Server with

Figure 1: The DokuWiki home page

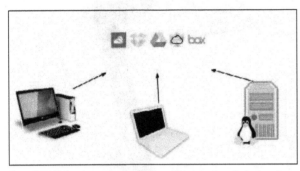

Figure 2: Multiple computers accessing the wiki content through cloud services

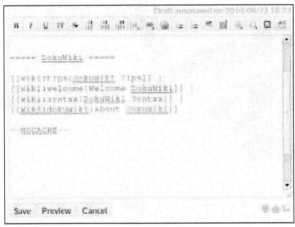

Figure 3: Page editor with markup toolbar

PHP language support. You do not need MySQL or any other database. XAMPP is a popular WAMP stack for the Windows operating system.

1. Download and install XAMPP (say, *C:\xampp*)
2. Download the DokuWiki zip file from *http://download.dokuwiki.org/* (e.g., *Downloads* directory)
3. Unzip the file
4. Copy the directory (and all sub-directories) 'dokuwiki' to *C:\xampp\htdocs*
5. You should see the following directory -- *C:\xampp\htdocs\dokuwiki*
6. Start Apache Server from XAMPP Control Panel
7. Go to *http://localhost/dokuwiki/* in the browser

8. You should see the DokuWiki home page

Note that all the wiki content you create will be under the directory *C:\xampp\htdocs\dokuwiki\data\pages*

You will see *start.txt* file under the directory which contains the welcome text.

Setup instructions are provided only for Windows, but the same instructions with a few changes (in the directory path) can help installation on Mac OS X and Linux platforms.

Sharing content across computers

Let us now set up a wiki such that you can access the content across multiple computers. Cloud storage services such as Google Drive have client software running as a service on Windows, Mac OS and Ubuntu (Grive). These client software ensure that the folder 'Google Drive' is always backed up in the cloud. The cloud stored files are available on different devices and get synced.

We can leverage this feature from the cloud service to link with DokuWiki. On Windows, the Google Drive application creates a folder with the name 'Google Drive' in the respective user's home directory. The client runs as a service and is visible in the tray as an icon. This service ensures the files are synced up with the cloud as and when changes happen.

DokuWiki expects the data files to be residing in *C:\xampp\htdocs\dokuwiki\data\pages*. You can create a link under this directory to the 'Google Drive' folder using the *mklink* command:

```
C:\xampp\htdocs\dokuwiki\data\pages> mklink /J gwiki <Google Drive directory>
```

You will see a link created under this directory named *gwiki*. This is the link name for the target Google Drive folder.

You additionally need to enable *FollowSymLinks* options in the Apache configuration file. This will ensure that the Apache Server allows the directory traversal below the *gwiki* directory through the symbolic link.

To start creating content to store under the *gwiki* directory, you can type 'gwiki:test' in the search bar. Since no page like that exists, you will be shown an option to 'Create this page'. You are now ready to create your first wiki page that gets stored in the cloud.

Similar linking of the Google Drive directory can be achieved on Mac OS X and Ubuntu systems using the link *(ln)* command.

Basic text editing in DokuWIki

DokuWIki comes with its own rules for formatting text, just like other wikis. It comes with a friendly editor toolbar that inserts the wiki syntax and lets you focus on content editing. While you can use text syntax like the '=' sign for a heading, it is convenient and advisable to use the format toolbar.

The first five buttons in the toolbar are for making text

Bold, Italics, Underline, Code text and *strike.*

Buttons with the H character are for headings. The first button in this series creates a heading of the same level as the previous one. This button is helpful when you are creating the outline of the document. For example, after the document title, which is H1, you create the first chapter with the H2 heading size. For the rest of the chapter, which will be at the same level (H2), you can just click this button.

To create a heading lower than the previous one, you need to select the second *Heading* button. To create a *heading* which is higher than the previous one, you should use the third *Heading* button. The fourth *Heading* button lets you create any heading from H1 to H6. Once you get used to the first three buttons, you will rarely use the fourth button.

Linking pages

The buttons with a chain link (shaped like the horizontal 8) are to be used to create links within the wiki pages and external Web pages. To link wiki pages already created, it is easy to click on the 'link' button and select the file from the pop-up.

When creating a new document, it is possible that the leaf pages are not yet created. You can create page links that are place holders, as follows:

```
[[wiki-page-test|Wiki Test Page]]
```

Editing sections

DokuWiki allows editing of sections of a Web page by focusing on the parts of the page being edited. Section edits are created automatically based on the *Heading* level.

Adding media

DokuWiki has a *Media Manager* to upload images and videos from the browser to the server for linking in documents later. You can create a document repository with links from the wiki.

Namespaces

Namespaces allow the grouping of pages. A namespace is similar to a directory. It makes for better organisation of wiki pages. For example, you could create one namespace for each team (to share common content) or for each subject (to take notes).

Referencing pages within the context of a namespace is simple. For example,

```
[[team-a:start| Team A Home]]
```

In the above example, *team-a* is the namespace and *start. txt* is the wiki page. Note that *.txt* extension is not required when referring to the wiki pages.

Version control

DokuWiki does version control of wiki pages. This helps to recover any content erased mistakenly. You can also see

Figure 4: Media Manager to view and upload media files

the difference between two versions with 'track changes'.

Recommended additions

The following additions are recommended in your DokuWiki.

Sidebar creation: Create a page name *'sidebar.txt'*. Give a list of high level links to your wiki homepage. This sidebar should reside in the *data/pages* directory.

Theme change: While the default theme 'dokuwiki' is good, a much better theme is *codowik*. This has a modern look-and-feel, and is responsive to screen dimensions across multiple screen resolutions.

To change the theme, follow the steps given below:
1. Go to the DokuWiki home page (see *References* section)
2. Search 'codowik' in the right side search bar
3. Click on 'codowik' (template)
4. Download
5. Unzip the downloaded file
6. Copy the directory codowik to *C:\xampp\htdocs\ dokuwiki\lib\tpl*
7. Open *C:\xampp\htdocs\dokuwiki\conf\local.php* file
8. Replace the *$conf*['template'] variable value with *'codowik'* (instead of *'dokuwiki'*)
9. Reload the DokuWiki page (*http://localhost/dokuwiki*)

If all the steps are followed, you should be able to see your start page with a new template.

Plugins: There are hundreds of add-ons for DokuWiki. Table 1 lists a few useful plugins you could try.

Table 1

Plugin	Functionality
calc	Inserts mathematical expressions and evaluates them on-the-fly
colour	Adds foreground and background colours to text. Helpful to highlight text.
todo	Adds *Task* list functionality to the wiki. *search-pattern* plugin also required for enhanced functionality of *todo* plugin.
vshare	Inserts video-embed links in wiki homepage
yearbox	Inserts year calendar in various formats and inserts notes against each date
wikical-endar	Monthly calendar display to add notes against each date

To install plugins, follow these steps:
1. Search for plugins based on their name (in the above table) in DokuWiki homepage
2. Download the zip file
3. Unzip the file in any temporary folder
4. Copy the unzipped directory to *C:\xampp\htdocs\ dokuwiki\lib\plugins*
5. For each plugin, there is a keyword that you need to insert in your wiki page. For more on the keyword and syntax, refer to the documentation on plugins. For example: *calc: 19.99*65=*

Further customisation

DokuWiki is highly customisable and no knowledge of programming is required. You can edit the values of various configuration variables in the file under *dokuwiki/conf*. The main configuration file is *dokuwiki.php* and *theslocal* file is appropriately named *local.php*

Some important customisation variables are given in Table 2.

Table 2

Variable	What it affects
$conf('title')	Wiki title
$conf('start')	Start page file name
$conf('sidebar')	Sidebar file name
$conf('savedir')	Directory where wiki (text) files are stored
$conf['toptoclevel']	Determines which level to include automatic 'Table of contents'
$conf['maxtoclevel']	Determines up to which heading level the 'Table of contents' should include
$conf['camelcase']	Should CamelCase (capitalising first word of letter) words be used for linking?
$conf['maxseclevel']	Up to which level the section should be editable

Figure 5: Layout with codowik template

For hosting a wiki in an intranet set-up, DokuWiki has user management and authentication plugins. Also, access control lists can be created with simple configuration changes.

If hosted in a local area network using a Wi-Fi home router, DokuWiki pages can be viewed and edited from a mobile (with a screen of 11.43 cm/4.5 inch or above) or iPad. The basic formatting and editing features have been tested and work well.

There are several advantages of shifting documentation creation from file-based proprietary formats (like DOC and One Note) to Web hosted browser-based editing software. Considering the simple setup and numerous features that DokuWiki offers, it is certainly worth reviewing for your personal and company needs. END

References

[1] DokuWiki Home *https://www.dokuwiki.org/dokuwiki*
[2] DokuWiki Syntax *https://www.dokuwiki.org/wiki:syntax*
[3] DokuWiki configuration *https://www.dokuwiki.org/config*

By: Janardan Revuru

The author is fond of productivity tools and spends time exploring open source software. For any queries on DokuWiki, he can be reached at *janardan.revuru@gmail.com*

Manage Your IT Infrastructure Effectively with Zentyal

Read about how Inmantec Institutions switched to Zentyal (formerly e-box Platform), which is a program for a Linux server and is meant for SMBs. Zentyal has a multi-faceted platform, as we will discover through this series.

Over the past many years, Inmantec Institutions had faced issues in managing its IT infrastructure. Problems included handling static IP pools for students and staff, managing Internet bandwidth such that it was not misused, etc. Here's a first hand account of how open source helped the institute manage its IT infrastructure efficiently and in a cost-effective manner.

For years, Inmantec used commercial software to manage its IT infrastructure. And like all proprietary software, this, too, did not provide the institution with a customised solution to manage the IP addresses of its students and staff, efficiently. In the case of static IP addresses, the institution was provided with four VLANs for all the staff and students of different courses. Most of the time, the organisation used IP addresses. These large static IP address pools had performance issues on commercial software. Inmantec required features like a captive portal, a DHCP server, real-time monitoring of users' downloads and uploads with statistics, etc. With all these issues to be addressed, different open source software were tested till Zentyal server was discovered. It resolved most of the problems.

Zentyal is a Linux-based business server, which is a replacement for Microsoft Small Business Server and Microsoft Exchange Server. The beauty of the software lies in its simplicity, short installation period and minimal maintenance. The features that attracted Inmantec to Zentyal were:

1. Communication Server, which has a mail server, groupware and instant messaging system.
2. Office Server, which contains an LDAP directory server, file sharing and domain services, printer sharing and backup facilities.
3. Systems Management, which is a software management utility and monitors hardware performance.
4. The infrastructure, which comprises a DHCP server, a DNS server, an NTP server, a certification authority, Apache Webserver, an FTP server and UPS management.

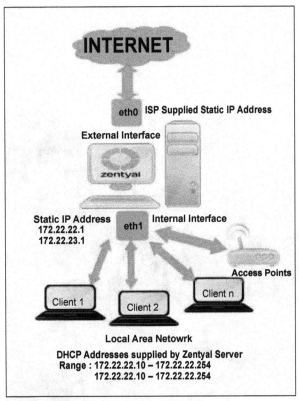

Figure 1: Setting up Zentyal for testing purposes

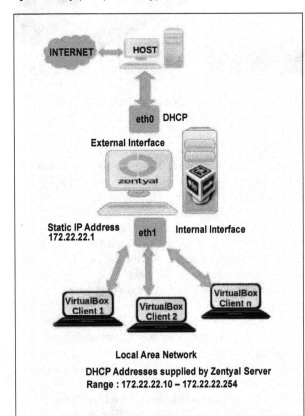

Figure 2: Dashboard used to control the server

5. Gateway and UTM, which has configurable network interfaces, high availability, advanced routing, an advanced firewall, traffic shaping and QOS, an advanced HTTP proxy server, a captive portal, a RADIUS server, VPN, an intrusion prevention system and mail filter.

Zentyal modules are customisable and can be handpicked at the time of installation. These features allow users to control most infrastructure management needs efficiently.

In this article, I will cover the setting up of Zentyal Server 3.4. We will explore two different scenarios—first a live scenario and then a test one. Those who do not have a spare server to use, can test run it on VirtualBox, which will be explained later.

Scenario 1: Setting up Zentyal on a production server

Hardware requirements:
- 32/64-bit hardware
- Two network interface cards
- 20 GB of hard disk space

Software requirements:
- Zentyal 3.4 32/64-bit server.

A server has two interface cards: eth0 and eth1. The interface eth0 is connected to the ISP, with a static address, and eth1 is connected to the LAN. The LAN interface is used to supply IP addresses to clients using a DHCP server. Interface eth1 is assigned two local IPs—72.22.22.1 and 172.22.23.1 in order to serve two VLANs (virtual LANs). Each IP address range has some IPs reserved for internal use, which can be assigned for internal servers, copiers, printers, etc, and the rest of the range can be assigned to clients. This range of IP addresses can serve up to 490 clients.

To provide IP addresses automatically to the clients in the network, we use a DHCP server. We also use a local domain so as to provide names to our devices. Names are easier to remember than IP addresses. So, if you want to access any device from the network, just use device name rather than IP address. We have set IAMT as our local domain name. We also use a captive portal, which will authenticate a user on the domain. This portal is also used to provide a download quota for each individual user. This quota is used as a limit for Internet bandwidth usage.

Scenario 2: Setting up Zentyal for testing purposes

Hardware requirements:
A 32/64-bit laptop/desktop, two virtual network interface cards, and 20 GB of hard disk space.

Software requirements:
Zentyal 3.4 32/64-bit server

Those who want to test this server on their local machines can use VirtualBox1 for testing purposes.

For VirtualBox, the Internet is shared with the host operating system; therefore, the primary virtual interface (eth0) of the guest Zentyal server operating system has to be set as DHCP and not static.

Installation of Zentyal Server

To set up Zentyal Server, follow the steps listed below:

1. Download Zentyal 3.4 from *http://zentyal.org.*
2. After downloading, burn the image on a CD. For VirtualBox, you can use the image directly.
3. Select the language—English.
4. You can install Zentyal with default settings by selecting 'Install Zentyal 3.4'. This step will install Zentyal via GUI and will delete all existing partitions on the hard disk. By selecting 'Expert mode' Zentyal can be installed in text mode.
5. Again, select the language required for the setup. In our case, its 'English.'
6. Choose your time zone settings. In our case, it's 'India'.
7. Choose the keyboard layout. In our case, it's 'No'.
8. Under 'Configure the keyboard' choose 'English US'.
9. Choose 'English US' for the 'Keyboard layout' too.
10. It will now detect hardware and start loading the additional components.
11. Choose 'eth0' as the primary network interface.
12. It will then configure the network interface. To set up the network interface manually, select 'Cancel' after IPv6 configuration. For VirtualBox, do not press anything.
13. Now choose 'Continue' to manually configure the network.
14. Now type in the IP address given by your ISP. This step is not required for VirtualBox users.
15. Type the netmask, as supplied by your ISP.
16. Provide the gateway, as supplied by your ISP.
17. Type the nameservers. In our case, we have used Google Open DNS. Do not use commas for more than one name server; use a space instead.
18. You will then be asked for the hostname. Type the 'Server Name' you want. The default is 'Zentyal'.
19. Next, you will be asked for the domain name. You can type any domain name like test.com or in my case, 'iamt'.
20. During installation, you will be asked for the username of the administrator of the system. Type any name.
21. Type the password for the administrator account and confirm the password.
22. The installation process will then begin. After the installation ends, the system will reboot.
23. After the system reboots, you will be asked to provide the username and password. After that, install modules for your server, click on the different modules available. We have selected all the modules. Click the 'Install' button to install the modules.
24. After installation process dashboard will appear.
     Setting up DHCP, DNS and the captive portal will be discussed in the next article. END

References

[1] VirtualBox Download: *https://www.virtualbox.org/wiki/Downloads*
[2] VirtualBox setup: *https://www.virtualbox.org/manual/ch01.html*
[3] Zentyal website: *http://www.zentyal.org*
[4] Google public DNS: *https://developers.google.com/speed/public-dns/*
[5] Zentyal installation: *http://doc.zentyal.org/en/installation.html*

By: Gaurav Parashar

The author is a FOSS enthusiast, and loves to work with open source technologies like Moodle and Ubuntu. He works as the Asst Dean (IT Studies), at Inmantec Institutions, Ghaziabad, UP. He can be reached at *gauravparashar24@gmail.com.*

Understanding SDT Markers and Debugging with Subtlety

Discover how to use Systemtap Dtrace style markers, which can be a great aid in a production environment to monitor the program flow.

D ebugging has become integral to a programmer's life. In C and C++, we normally debug using *printf()s/ couts, gdb, valgrind*, etc. SDT markers are very handy due to their simplicity yet great debugging capabilities.

What are SDT markers?
The abbreviation stands for 'Systemtap Dtrace' style markers. They are statically placed user space markers which can later be probed *dynamically* for some useful information.

Why use them?
SDT markers are normally placed at important spots in programs and can later be probed for some useful information; for instance, if you want to determine the code flow, the values of some important variables, etc. This information is what we look for while debugging.

SDT markers are being quite widely used now. For example, applications/libraries like PostgreSQL, MySQL,

Mozilla, Perl, Python, Java, Ruby, libvirt, QEMU, glib, etc have these markers embedded in them. Most of us aren't even aware of them but a quick scan of a standard Fedora 20 system will show a total of over 4000 SDT markers. However, this may not be true for other distros.

How to use SDT markers
Using SDT markers is very simple. You have to include the *<sys/sdt.h>* header in your program. If this header file is absent, then install the *systemtap-sdt-devel* package for Fedora, RedHat and related distros. For distros like Ubuntu and Debian, the package name is *systemtap-sdt-dev*. After including the header file, you just have to use a variant of the macro *STAP_PROBE (provider_name, marker_name)* wherever you want the marker to be placed.

The arguments *provider_name* and *marker_name* are very important. They establish the identity of the marker. Here is a simple example to show how SDT markers are used:

```
#include <stdio.h>
#include <sys/sdt.h>     /* Include this header file */

int main(void)
{
    printf("In main\n");

    STAP_PROBE(test, in_main);

    return 0;
}
```

Figure 1: *stap* waiting for the marker to be hit

Using them is fairly simple. Also, compilation doesn't involve any tricks. Just the same old:

```
$ gcc test.c -o test
```

Let's probe and trace the markers.

Probing and tracing markers with Systemtap

Using SDT markers won't give us anything unless we probe and trace them. For this, we need a tool called Systemtap.

Systemtap, developed by RedHat, is a very powerful debugging and performance analysis tool that's widely used these days. You need to install the packages *systemtap* and *systemtap-runtime*. In Fedora and RedHat-based systems, run the following command:

```
yum install systemtap systemtap-runtime
```

If you face any problems with the installation and usage, go to the site: *https://sourceware.org/systemtap/* and access the beginners' guide, which shouldn't be very hard to follow. User space probing functionality takes help from the *uprobes* infrastructure which has been present in the kernel since kernel version 3.5. To check your kernel version, use the following command:

```
$ uname -r
```

And to check if the *uprobes* functionality is available, use:

```
$ grep CONFIG_UPROBES  /boot/config-`uname -r`
```

…which should show you the following:

```
CONFIG_UPROBES=y
```

After you make sure that Systemtap is installed, open another terminal to run *stap*.

In one terminal, issue the following code:

```
# stap -v -e 'probe process("/home/user/test").mark("in_
```

Figure 2: *test* runs three times and marker was hit three times

```
main") { printf("Marker in_main Hit\n"); }'
```

What we have done here is run a Systemtap script from the command line mentioning that we need to probe executable with path as */home/user/test*, and the marker we need to probe into is *in_main*. And if control hits the marker, we must display *Marker in_main Hit*. The option *-e* is to instruct *stap* that we are providing the script on the command line itself and *-v* is to display a verbose output.

Run this command and you will find that after five passes (refer to Figure 1), it just waits—for the program to be run and the marker to be hit. So, in another terminal, run the program with the marker and see the result in the terminal running Systemtap (refer to Figure 2).

How does this help? You can place these markers (any number of them) in programs to determine the code flow. One can argue that it would be much simpler to use *printf()* s instead of these markers to determine the code flow. But every time you run the program, a lot of unnecessary data is displayed. We don't want that, nor do we want to interfere with the program's output. We want the data to be displayed only when we need it. SDT markers are dormant. They can never do anything on their own. Only when somebody needs more information, the markers can be probed with tools like Systemtap to find out the details.

SDT markers with arguments

Only finding out the hits on SDT markers isn't enough.

Figure 3: *test* runs three times with three different values, after which, see the output

Figure 4: *.readelf* output showing the *.stapsdt.base* and the *.note.stapsdt* sections (*ALLOC* bit is turned off for *.note.stapsdt*)

Let's get some more information at a particular point in the program about some important variables. That's where the arguments come to the fore. Here is a simple program showing their usage:

```
#include <stdio.h>
#include <sys/sdt.h>

int main(void)
{
    int no;
    printf(
    scanf("%d", &no);

    STAP_PROBE1(test, input, no);
    if (no > 5) {
```

```
        STAP_PROBE(test, greater);
        foo();
    } else {
        STAP_PROBE(test, lesser);
        fun();
    }
}
```

In the above code snippet, we have used three markers. Again, the program isn't important but the usage of the marker is. See the first one: *STAP_PROBE1*. Notice '1' as the suffix? This specifies that you are sending one argument, which in this case is *no*. Similarly, if we use two arguments, then the suffix would be '2'. It can go on till 12. After that, you have to specify N for N number of arguments. For more information on this, skim through <sys/sdt.h>.

Now, compile the program. This time, let's write a script for Systemtap to be executed in a file (not in the command line). Systemtap scripts should end with *.stp*. Here is the script:

```
probe process("/home/hemant/backup/home_backup/prac/
test").mark("input") {
    printf("input marker hit and value = %d\n",
$arg1);
}
probe process("/home/hemant/backup/home_backup/prac/
test").mark("greater") {
    printf("Marker <greater> hit, call to foo()\n");
}
probe process("/home/hemant/backup/home_backup/prac/
test").mark("lesser") {
    printf("Marker <lesser> hit, call to fun()\n");
}
```

Systemtap uses C-style statements like *printf()*. The first probe point is important. We are asking Systemtap to print the value *$arg1*. If we had to use more arguments, then we would have used *$arg2*, *$arg3*, etc, to retrieve those values. To run this script, use:

```
$ stap -v script.stp
```

You can refer to Figure 3. Remember to run the program in another terminal. We can also send a string pointer as an argument and print that in the script. You are free to try that.

Here's a look at what happens behind the scenes.

Location of SDT markers in the ELF

The standard format for object code in Linux is Executable and Linkable Format (ELF). We know that an ELF consists of sections (like the *.data*, *.rodata*, *.text*, etc). When we compile a program containing SDT markers, two sections called *.note.stapsdt* and *.base.stapsdt* are created (sometimes, three sections including *.probes,* but that's only if we use semaphores). How does it happen? Well, if you look closely into the *<sys/sdt.h>*, the preprocessor converts the *STAP_PROBE()* macro variants into *asm* directives. This can be verified using the C preprocessor command *cpp.*

The *asm* directives help in creating these sections (*.note.stapsdt* and *.base.stapsdt*) and embedding the information about the markers into them.

The important section is *.note.stapsdt* which contains the information about all the SDT markers, like their name, provider, location in the object code, etc. Let us look at the first program (containing a single marker) shown earlier, as an example.

Compile that program:

```
$ gcc test.c -o test
```

Now, use the command *readelf* to see if those sections were created:

```
$ readelf -S ./test
```

Refer to Figure 4.

We can clearly see the section *.note.stapsdt* present. To view the contents of this section, one can either use *objdump -dt ./test* and then look for this section and its contents, or the much subtler way is to use *readelf* to read all the notes' information. SDT markers are actually *notes* with type as *stapsdt.*

Note that the ALLOC bits for the section *.note.stapsdt* are set off. That means this section won't be loaded into memory when the program is loaded to run. How does this help? If we have a large number of SDT markers being used, this might take up a large amount of space in the memory; hence, it's better not to load it.

```
$readelf -n ./test
```

The output in Figure 5 displays information about all the notes present in that program. The last one is an SDT note. We know that because we can see that the owner of that note is *stapsdt.* SDT notes have *stapsdt* as their owner. That defines their type.

Here, we find the type of note, provider name, marker name, the location in the program and some other information including a semaphore address. Let's ignore the semaphore address for now. The location shown here is 0x40053e. If, in the object code we find the instruction at the following address:

```
$ objdump -dt ./test | grep 40053e
```

...the instruction at this address will be *nop,* as shown in Figure 6.

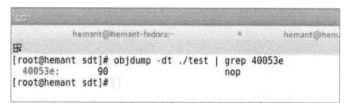

Figure 5: *stapsdt* is the SDT note

```
[root@hemant sdt]# objdump -dt ./test | grep 40053e
  40053e:        90                        nop
[root@hemant sdt]#
```

Figure 6: *nop* is stored at the location of the SDT note

So, the place at which we placed our marker has been replaced with a *nop.* This can also be seen from the assembler directives which replace the macro *STAP_PROBE()* where a *nop* instruction is placed. And since the SDT markers are replaced with *nop's,* they are dormant (when not being probed).

Probing that location

When we probe the marker using Systemtap, the section *.note.stapsdt* is retrieved. From this section, the information about all the SDT notes/markers is also retrieved. After obtaining the information about the note, the location of the SDT marker and the executable path is sent to the kernel's *uprobes* interface. It replaces the *nop* instruction with an *int3* instruction, which is a trap (refer to Figure 7).

This interrupt is handled by a default handler in the kernel. But this is where the Systemtap again interferes. The Systemtap script we write is converted into a kernel module, which is loaded into the kernel as soon as the script is run, using *stap.*

Systemtap creates its own handler for *uprobes* (present in the kernel module) to record the necessary data like arguments, values, etc, and hence, displays it to us. So, for each hit on the event, this handler gets called and the required action is taken (the action being specified in the script we write).

I won't go into the details of Systemtap due to space limitations. One can always find documentation regarding Systemtap.

So, whenever control reaches the marker location (currently being probed) in a program, it hits *int3.* The interrupt handler for *int3* gets called and, sequentially, all the

Figure 7: Comparison of the runtime images of the ELF before and after placement of probe point (ouput obtained using *gdb disas*)

Figure 8: Steps to use *uprobes* interface *trace* file is empty

events mentioned above take place.

Tracing without Systemtap

Now, let's trace and probe manually using *uprobes* directly!

First, find out the mount point of *debugfs*. This virtual subsystem exists only in memory. We can find that out by using:

```
$ mount | grep debugfs
```

In Figure 8, we find that it is */sys/kernel/debugfs*.

This contains a *tracing* directory and there are a few available tracers. We need the *nop* tracer.

```
# echo nop > /sys/kernel/debug/tracing/current_tracer
```

In one terminal, let's find out the location of the marker we want to trace using the same *readelf*.

Let's suppose it is 0x40053e. Feed this address to *uprobe_events* in the tracing directory:

```
# echo "p:user/in_main ./test:0x53e" > /sys/kernel/debug/
```

tracing/uprobe_events

Note that we are probing on 0x53e and not on 0x40053e. The *.text* section in x86 starts at 0x400000 and this is taken care of by the *uprobes* interface. So just subtract 0x400000 from the note location we retrieved using *readelf*. In the context of *uprobes*, user is an event group and *in_main* is an event.

After making this entry, a directory named *user* is created in the *events* subdirectory inside the *tracing* directory. This corresponds to a group of events, of which, one event is *in_main*.

Clear out the *trace* file:

```
# echo > /sys/kernel/debug/tracing/trace
```

Let's enable the event we want to trace, as follows:

```
# echo 1 > /sys/kernel/debug/tracing/events/user/
enable
```

In this case, we are enabling the complete event group which doesn't make a difference.

Start tracing, as follows:

```
# echo 1 > /sys/kernel/debug/tracing/tracing_on
```

The tracing has begun. Now, just run the program in another terminal and then let's look at the trace:

```
# cat /sys/kernel/debug/tracing/trace
```

It shows the task, its PID, the timestamp when the hit was recorded and the event name we are trying to trace. It also shows the hits (refer to Figure 9).

The arguments' support is not yet present in the kernel. But this support is being integrated and will soon be available, presumably in the next kernel version.

This article will just familiarise you with SDT markers and their importance, giving you a little insight into their probing and tracing. It's up to you as to how you use them. Their importance can be gauged by the fact that QEMU uses over 500 markers. They can also be used in network programs to see the data received at the client's or at the server side. Libvirt uses them before making the RPC calls, so that if we probe on these markers, we will be able to know the data being sent and received. If you face any problem, just probe them, find out the relevant data and find out the source. END

By: Hemant Kumar Shaw

The author is a Linux user, an open source enthusiast and a contributor.

For Bizosys Technologies, FOSS is the Gateway to Success

Bengaluru-based Bizosys Technologies has developed a Hadoop-based search engine that now drives the company's growth.

The Bizosys team at work in the Bengaluru office

Who says that a good business model cannot be based on open source software? The classic case of Bizosys Technologies clearly demonstrates that open source can play a key role in a company's growth. Bizosys Technologies Pvt Ltd was started in 2009 with the broad intent of combining all the knowledge built up across an enterprise, especially the rapidly growing unstructured information in the varied forms of documents, media, log files and emails—spanning collaboration, communication and information systems. At that point, most data-driven businesses were focused on structured data in ERP, CRM and traditional database systems.

Giving wings to 'open' ideas

The co-founders of Bizosys had met while working at Infosys. Sunil Guttula, an engineering graduate from IIT Kharagpur, is the CEO and manages overall growth, finance and sales at Bizosys. Abinash Karan from NIT, Rourkela, is the CTO and manages product development, engineering, support and customer solutions. Sridhar Dhulipala is a product design graduate from NID, Ahmedabad, and manages the product management, user experience and marketing functions. "To create a solution that looked at both structured and unstructured data was our broad focus, and from that effort emerged Bizosys' first product in 2010. HSearch is a Hadoop-based search engine that not only addresses the scale required in dealing with large volumes of structured and unstructured data, but also provides real-time performance capabilities. HSearch was built on top of available open source software from Apache like HBase, Lucene, etc, to enhance Hadoop for scale and performance. Hadoop-based HSearch comfortably deals

> "HSearch is deployed as a big data store and is a more economical alternative to in-memory cache or traditional database-driven solutions. HSearch is central to Bizosys' business and the firm's entire business comes from it, the core engine of which is an Apache licensed product"

with data volumes over 10 terabytes, yet queries are served within sub-second response times," explains Dhulipala.

HSearch was released as an OSS contribution from Bizosys under the liberal Apache 2.0 licence via Sourceforge in November 2010. There have been over 2000 developer downloads from 80+ countries worldwide over the past 3.5 years, with India, China, United States, Korea and Germany being the countries that logged the highest downloads. HSearch was benchmarked for its performance in May 2011 at Intel Labs.

FOSS: The scalable business model

Bizosys' business model comprises a mix of professional services and solutions development. Two of the company's subsequent offerings were in the data preparation/harvesting and real-time predictive analytics space. They leverage the open nature of HSearch, but include additional libraries and code that are specific to data extraction and transformation, as well as algorithms for predictive analytics applied to time-series data. These two solutions are commercial offerings. In its third commercial offering, HSearch is deployed as a big data store and is a more economical alternative to in-memory cache or traditional database-driven solutions.

HSearch is central to Bizosys' business and the firm's entire business comes from it, the core engine of which is an Apache licensed product, says Dhulipala.

HSearch is built on top of existing OSS products, primarily from Apache Foundation, to make Hadoop, which is a batch-oriented solution, into a real-time solution. Several enhancements bring it closer to enterprise requirements in terms of the scale, performance levels and security that it offers, on the IT side. And for business, rapid search, data exploration and analysis is what HSearch offers. Through its engagements with large and small enterprises, Bizosys has found that the number of organisations looking at open source and NoSQL offerings, for the benefits that products like HSearch and Hadoop address, is growing rapidly. "Product companies, primarily in the analytics space, that are confronted with the challenges of large volumes of unstructured data, query performance response times, etc, are also looking at the emerging Hadoop and NoSQL ecosystem for solutions. One CIO of a billion dollar group told Bizosys, 'I want my data to be more 'analysable'.' There has

been an explosion in an organisation's own internal data — a surfeit of machine data, meta data, emails and user-generated content, etc," quips Dhulipala.

According to him, these companies are looking at startups to provide them with innovative solutions. "A large financial MNC has launched an internal initiative that actively seeks to replace any COTS product with an OSS product, wherever suitable. OSS software companies such as Red Hat, etc, have set the right precedent by making OSS acceptable to enterprise IT. HSearch from Bizosys is not an exception here, and serves its own target audience in the big data space by having a core OSS offering," adds Dhulipala.

For Bizosys, adopting OSS from organisations such as the Apache Foundation was clearly an engineering and business choice. From the engineering perspective, Hadoop evolved from addressing non-enterprise problems (having emerged out of a Google paper). As a business decision, being a startup, Bizosys was keen on keeping its operating expenses low so OSS was the best choice, especially under a liberal Apache licence. And it was also keen on contributing back in some measure. HSearch was, in fact, a contribution made back to the community even before Bizosys arrived at its current business model.

A growth story for others to emulate

So what has Bizosys' growth been like over the past few years? Are there plans for expansion in the near future? "The last two years have been more business focused – we plan to grow as an advanced analytics company in the big data space offering superior scale and performance advantages for customers. Bizosys is currently focused on strengthening its sales side to achieve aggressive topline revenue growth. And through targeted engagements, the firm plans to enhance HSearch with new features or functions that add value to the core product," says Dhulipala.

And how does it work — does the company approach a firm and counsel them to try its open source solutions or is it the other way round? How does Bizosys convince an IT manager or a CIO who's wondering if this is the right time to deploy open source solutions? Dhulipala elaborates, "The advantage of going with an OSS approach is that, in certain situations, we found that the client side IT team was already aware of HSearch (to our surprise) and that helped build the credibility factor. In fact, in one meeting facilitated by our partner, Microsoft Azure, when the HSearch slide came up, the prospect asked us to skip it as his team was aware of it!"

Anecdotes apart, OSS is a key part of Bizosys' strategy, primarily because it removes the conflict of interests when discussing IT solutions with customers. "Clients are assured that the product that best serves their requirements or the use case at hand, will be used," shares Dhulipala.

Bizosys has worked with legal experts specialising

in the software field to draft contracts such as the Master Services Agreement, etc, to clearly demarcate who owns the intellectual property. All the work specifically developed for a client remains its IP. The remaining IP that comes from OSS is considered 'background IP' with no exclusive rights provided to the client, allowing those pieces, libraries, etc, to be used in multiple situations for different clients and for the benefit of the OSS community, especially developers.

For a client, there is a strong business case for adopting OSS because of the reduced CAPEX involved, especially with reliable products that come with robust source code and documentation.

So are most of Bizosys' customers adopting open source software along with proprietary applications, or are they replacing the later completely? "In the Big Data space, there are new robust solutions such as SAP HANA that have made inroads into the in-memory solutions domain to deal with the volume, velocity, variety of data that firms need to deal with. These are seen as complementary solutions to existing, monolithic systems that are very expensive to scale, and even then do not match HANA's scale or performance. HSearch is a disk-based solution and clearly can be an alternative. We don't see customers replacing their existing core systems, ERP solutions, etc, entirely, but adding OSS solutions to complement their existing IT investments. Sure, there are smaller, niche systems that may be replaced entirely, such as log management software where scale is a huge challenge; and large historical data stores where alerting is critical, especially as the external environment changes in terms of competition or regulations. OSS adoption is likely to continue on a complementary basis in most cases, and for specific niche situations, might be replacing the proprietary software used earlier," says Dhulipala.

The bottlenecks in adopting FOSS

Dhulipala has a lot to say about the challenges faced by firms that sell open source solutions. While elaborating on the toughest hurdle his team has faced so far, he says, "Evangelising and spreading the word, followed by building a solid, active community of users, are the challenges. Currently, there is no one platform to find and enrol evangelists or developers—one has to depend on blogs. Besides, a majority of OSS is often created by smaller teams with little or no funding, except for the rare Cloudera or Hortonworks, the developers of which managed to raise millions for their model or distribution of Hadoop. Second, it's a challenge to find sharp developers who share your vision of the OSS product, its roadmap and are willing to become 'committers'. The single largest challenge in building a vibrant OSS community is finding the evangelists and committers."

And what does he feel is the biggest hurdle in the adoption of open source solutions at the enterprise

level? Dhulipala replies, "The single biggest hurdle is often support, followed by the solution's ease of use. Developers often are required to either think differently or master new skills when it comes to several OSS products, especially in the NoSQL space. Next, the credibility of the OSS solution comes into play. A good number of successful deployments in the particular industry that the prospective client belongs to, also helps in adoption. These challenges become harder in highly regulated industries such as finance and insurance, where there might be viable OSS alternatives hypothetically that could be stitched together to form a core banking solution, for instance, but lack of deployments prevents adoption. On the other hand, cost-sensitive industries in highly competitive segments would gladly look for an OSS solution for certain functions."

Interaction with the community and the days ahead

Regarding Bizosys' involvement with the open source community at the global level, Dhulipala shares, "There are two ways we have engaged with the OSS community — sharing our work via popular forums such as Microsoft Teched, Yahoo Hadoop Summit, Hasgeek Fifth Elephant, and several of the emerging local meet-ups that are less formal in nature. The source code for HSearch is itself available via a dedicated website *www.hadoopsearch.net* maintained currently by Bizosys, and also on Github and Sourceforge."

So what are the innovative solutions that Bizosys' is working on at present? "Bizosys is a Big Data advanced analytics company that sees its growth coming from the constant, rapid increase in data volumes, both structured and unstructured. Today, user generated content and machine log data are primary contributors to the high volumes, e.g., social feeds and metadata on a huge number of monitored events. Tomorrow, this is likely to grow even more with the IoT or Internet of Things scenario. Against this backdrop, Bizosys sees its solutions' ability to deal with the twin demands of scale and performance as its key strength, and its roadmap is based on strengthening offerings that fundamentally address this challenge. We will address the packaging of these solutions, from a business standpoint, whether it is real-time predictive analytics on streaming data or a cost-effective and smarter data store to manage petabytes of data and more. As businesses prepare to deal with data-driven challenges in terms of analytics, operations, customer experience or plain growth and differentiation, Bizosys expects to align its business and industry-specific solutions more finely to these challenges. All along, we expect OSS to be core to our business strategy," concludes Dhulipala. END

By Priyanka Sarkar

The author is a member of the editorial team. She loves to weave in and out the little nuances of life and scribble her thoughts and experiences in her personal blog.

10 OPEN SOURCE APPS THAT RUN ON WINDOWS

There are a number of applications in the open source world that are free to use. Many of them perform better than their proprietary counterparts. In this article, the author gives a list of alternatives to proprietary software, covering office productivity tools, browsers, vector art and image editing tools.

Linux is a wonderful operating system and comes with almost everything that a user might require. However, sometimes you might just have to use MS Windows, even though you'd prefer not to — for instance, if your office primarily works with Windows, or you are a gaming fan and prefer to retain MS Windows to play the latest action games. But did you know that even in such cases you can use open source software as alternatives to closed source proprietary options?

Using open source tools and software on MS Windows serves a dual purpose: on one hand, you get the satisfaction of supporting open source and freedom, and on the other hand, you can also save a good deal of money by not relying on highly overpriced proprietary tools.

So let's acquaint ourselves with some of the common and most popular open source alternatives to proprietary software.

1. Libre Office (an alternative to Microsoft Office)

If you are looking for an office and productivity suite that does not burn a hole in your pocket, look no further than Libre Office.

Much like Microsoft Office, Libre Office, too, comes loaded with many tools, including a word processor, a drawing tool, spreadsheet software, a database management application, and so on. However, unlike Microsoft Office, Libre Office is totally free and open source.

Libre Office is cross-platform, and it runs equally well on Linux, Mac and, of course, Windows!

Website: *http://www.libreoffice.org/*

2. Inkscape (an alternative to Adobe Illustrator and CorelDRAW)

Inkscape is a powerful vector graphics editor that offers a wide array of features, including alpha blending, markers, and so on.

If you are someone who works often with Scalable Vector Graphics (SVG), you probably rely mostly on Adobe Illustrator and CorelDRAW. While both these programs are handy tools, Inkscape offers an equally powerful and intuitive solution; yet, it is totally open source and free.

Website: *http://inkscape.org/*

3. The GIMP (an alternative to Adobe Photoshop)

The GNU Image Manipulation Program, or the GIMP as it is commonly called, is a very capable and robust image editor. An easy-to-use photo editor, it can double up as a versatile image retouching tool for advanced users, offering features such as batch image processing, image format conversion, etc.

As with most open source software and unlike Adobe Photoshop, the GIMP is free. It is also cross-platform and supports various operating systems, including MS Windows.

Website: *www.gimp.org*

4. Blender (an alternative to 3DS Max and LightWave 3D)

When it comes to rendering 3D objects and for animation, Blender is one tool that can outshine costly proprietary alternatives in every aspect.

As a 3D content creation suite, Blender supports modelling, animation, rendering, and even comes with a detailed and powerful game engine. Several movies and other projects have been created using Blender, and the software is in no way weaker than its proprietary counterparts.

Website: *http://www.blender.org/*

5. BRL-CAD (an alternative to AutoCAD)

BRL-CAD is a cross-platform open source modelling tool. It has been under active development for well over two decades.

As a modelling tool, BRL-CAD offers geometric analysis, ray tracing, interactive editing, image processing, and several other features.

Website: *http://brlcad.org/*

6. Mozilla Thunderbird (an alternative to Microsoft Outlook)

If you use a desktop mail client to manage your email, opting for the rather costly and bulky Microsoft Outlook isn't your only option. You can try Mozilla Thunderbird, a free desktop email client that is fully open source.

As a matter of fact, Thunderbird is way better than Outlook in several aspects, such as being lightweight and offering better contact management tools. If you haven't done so already, you should by all means give Mozilla Thunderbird a spin!

Website: *http://www.mozilla.org/en-US/thunderbird/*

7. Chromium and/or Mozilla Firefox (alternatives to MS Internet Explorer, Opera and Safari)

Let's face it—when it comes to browsing the Web, the world has already dumped Microsoft Internet Explorer. Other closed source browsers such as Safari, too, are not the most popular options out there.

The world's leading Web browsers, for that matter, are open source. Chromium (the browser that serves as the base for Google Chrome) and Mozilla Firefox are Web browsers that should definitely be on your system. Whatever it is that you want—data sync, faster Web browsing or a better overall online experience—these two Web browsers will not disappoint you!

Websites: *http://www.mozilla.org/en-US/firefox/* *http://www.chromium.org/Home*

8. 7-Zip (an alternative to WinZip and WinRAR)

7-Zip is a file compression tool that comes with a GPL licence. It supports numerous file formats, and offers a compression ratio that is roughly 10 per cent better than that of WinZip.

7-Zip has been localised into 70+ languages and it offers AES-256 encryption. Besides, 7-Zip integrates well with the Windows shell, so you can use its features easily.

Website: *http://www.7-zip.org/*

9. Dia (an alternative to Microsoft Visio)

Dia is a lightweight diagram editor that is available for both Linux and Windows. It supports various standard formats, such as EPS and SVG. Dia offers a no-nonsense interface that lets you work on your drawings with ease.

Website: *http://dia-installer.de/*

10. VLC Media Player (an alternative to Windows Media Player, Real Player, ZOOM Player, etc)

VLC is a free, open source and cross-platform multimedia player that plays almost every media file. It works with DVDs, CDs and multimedia files, and offers advanced features such as video/audio encoding, file format processing, and so on.

Also worth a look is Miro (http://www.getmiro.com/) for videos and Kantaris (http://kantaris.org/) for audio.

Website: *http://www.videolan.org/vlc/index.html*

Irrespective of the operating system that you are running, you can always make use of handy open source tools and software that are not just robust and powerful but also offer an intuitive and easy-to-use interface. These open source tools are invariably well supported by an active community and helpful documentation. Thus, even if you are an MS Windows user, you should give some of the open source tools a try. You certainly will not be disappointed, and you're definitely not going to miss the proprietary alternatives! **END**

By: Sufyan bin Uzayr

The author is a Linux enthusiast and the editor of an e-journal named 'Brave New World' (*www.bravenewworld.in*). His primary areas of interest include open source, mobile development, Web CMS and vector art. Sufyan blogs at *www.sufyanism.com* and on Facebook at *www.facebook.com/sufyanism*

"The IoT is great, but comes with security challenges for developers"

The time has come for embedded Linux to rule. From consumer electronics (like set-top boxes and smart TVs), in-vehicle infotainment (IVI), networking equipment (wireless routers) and industrial automation, to spacecraft flight software and medical instruments, embedded Linux offers endless possibilities. Android has pushed the frontiers of this domain to an entirely new level with devices getting launched every other day. But though the use of embedded Linux is growing, there are challenges that it faces. The biggest one, perhaps, is the need for stronger security capabilities.

Open Source For You spoke to *Alok Mehrotra, country manager (India) and Rajesh Lalwani, account manager, Wind River* about how the company's 'security profile' helps combat the everyday threats that are a normal offshoot of the Internet of Things (IoT). Excerpts:

Q Do brief us about Wind River's presence in the open source domain.

I'd like to share a little bit of history with you. VxWorks is our real time operating system (RTOS). You will find that pretty much any mission-critical embedded design you can think of will be on an RTOS, and that RTOS will typically be Wind River. To give you some perspective, today, we have over one and a half billion devices running on Wind River as the operating system, on which you go ahead and build your applications.

Commercial embedded Linux continues to gain traction across the board as the aerospace, defence, industrial, networking and automotive industries see how open source encourages rapid innovation at far lower costs. But navigating the open source ecosystem is not an easy task, and Linux is different from the real time operating systems, software development tools and test frameworks that play a critical role in developing and deploying embedded devices. Thanks to the thousands of developers who strive to make it better, Linux constantly evolves and expands over time.

Currently, we are experiencing the Internet of Things (IoT) phenomenon, where everything is connected to everything else. It's an amazing concept. However, the major challenge is how to secure the network using open source technology, which is available to everybody. In a nutshell, the IoT is great, but it comes with a few security challenges for developers.

Wind River has come up with a security profile on top of

Alok Mehrotra, country manager (India), Wind River

Linux, which secures the operating system besides being Evaluation Assurance Levels-4 (EAL-4) certified. It's a commercial off-the-shelf (COTS) product, built to align with the Common Criteria for Operating System Protection Profile. In this, we've hardened the kernel, enhanced the user space and have given the entire control of the user space to the super user. The security-focused kernel includes features like grsecurity, PaX and enhanced Address Space Layout Randomisation (ASLR), among others.

Q What are the complex issues that developers face with the Internet of Things (IoT)?

Everybody has their own definition for the Internet of Things. Connectivity, manageability and security are important aspects. To me, the bigger question from the IoT perspective is not just how I connect to an aggregator, but how does this whole thing happen with the edge of the cloud.

The IoT has various applications such as smart cities, for instance, where the concept can be widely implemented with connected cars. Industrial automation is another application, where everything you need is on the Internet, so you can regularly update it. In the aforementioned cases, you need various protocols since you want everything to be secure, and these must be connected on the cloud as well. We need security at two levels. One, so that nobody can attack your system, and two, so that nobody can install their own application on top of it. In case they want to install a particular application, they need to have some authorised access to it.

Q How would you differentiate between enterprise and embedded Linux?

When you refer to embedded Linux, it's got one kernel that anybody can download from kernel.org. It then becomes enterprise Linux or embedded Linux depending on the kind of application you're developing. When you install it on any normal PC, you call it enterprise Linux, but when you use the same kernel for all your embedded applications—mobiles, connected homes, in-vehicle infotainment (IVI), etc, it becomes embedded Linux.

Q Security has emerged as one of the key considerations while developing products and solutions for all companies today, as seen in the case of the recent Heartbleed episode. What are your thoughts on this?

Let's assume that the largest network equipment provider in the world is building a fairly critical application and, that too, on Linux. Assume that there are millions of people who will get impacted if there is a bug in the operating system used. The application needs 99.99999 uptime. The company also needs a team that is ahead of the curve from an open source perspective, but that team still needs to work with a vendor that is conversant in open source and Linux. The vendor has to ensure that any issues found anywhere get patched and fixed in a manner such that the network equipment company is protected and is able to deliver to its customers. I was recently reading some information that was being circulated within Wind River. Heartbleed became known to the public

Rajesh Lalwani, account manager, Wind River

"Many IVIs out there are Android-based and we have a very strong presence in the domain. We are one of the founding members of the Open Handset Alliance (OHA), something that came up even before Android became what it is today!"

on 7th April (in Finnish) and 8th April (in English). A fix was available on OLS to our Wind River Linux customers for download on 8th April - less than 24 hours after Heartbleed was introduced to the public domain. If you're running anything that has some level of criticality, you would absolutely need to have that level of security.

Q Can Android challenge embedded Linux?

If you look at the Android kernel, it's a flavour of Linux. There's no challenge as such. The only thing is that there must be interoperability between Android and Linux. Android is being used extensively on the enterprise side—in mobiles, particularly. Now, to explain embedded Linux, let's look at routers. Here, most things run on VxWorks, or any other RTOS, but you cannot use Android. On the application side, Android is being used on the mobile, tablet or on a few of the IVIs that are coming out.

Many IVIs out there are Android-based and we have a very strong presence in the domain. We are one of the founding members of the Open Handset Alliance (OHA), something that came up even before Android became what it is today!

Q Do you have some engagement opportunities for engineers?

Some of our core Indian customers came to us and expressed their concern about the fact that they were not getting trained engineers to work on our technology. We discussed this issue internally and came out with university licences. We now give the same technology provided by us commercially at a much subsidised price to universities. At the same time, we offer them a programme called Train the Trainer (TTT) to help train faculty members. We also provide them with a curriculum, if they ask for one. We are currently working with a number of key organisations that are writing a curriculum for Indian engineering colleges. END

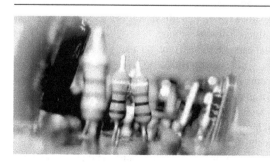

HTC Launches Three New Smartphones for the Indian Market

Taiwanese smartphone maker HTC recently launched its brand new Android-powered smartphone—the HTC One (M8). With it came an array of developer initiatives. *Faisal Siddiqui, Country Head, HTC,* spoke to *Prasid Banerjee* from *Open Source For You* about the new SDKs, its new models targeting the mid-range and budget segment, as well as HTC's commitment to the Indian market.

Faisal Siddiqui, Country Head, HTC

W ith its newest smartphone out in the market, it seems that HTC has made some important changes. For one, the company, which has been known to put high price tags on its devices, has come up with a high but strategic pricing for its new flagship model. In addition, the company has a lot to offer developers, who can lay their hands on a couple of juicy SDKs.

The M8 comes with Sense 6, a new version of the HTC's smartphone user interface. For the first time, the Sense UI comes with an open SDK and the company is inviting developers to work their magic. "By opening the SDK, we're expanding the scope of Sense 6. There are a lot of things that developers can come up with, which we may not think of," said Siddiqui.

The Sense UI indeed offers a lot of scope to developers. The Blinkfeed, which is one of its primary components, can easily be a developer's dream. For the uninitiated, the Blinkfeed is a compilation of your entire social network, news and some other apps. It gives you easy access to them. The SDK can be obtained from the company's developer website and developers only need to approach HTC.

The Sense UI isn't the only new open SDK though. The highlight of HTC's new device is its dual camera lenses, which have made way for some attractive new features. The addition of the second lens, which resides above the regular camera lens, gives the user features like copy/pasting elements from a picture. This means you can pick up elements from one photo and insert them in another. It has other features too, like refocusing an image after it has been clicked. While the camera is still the 4 Ultrapixel model that was seen on the HTC One, the company's developer site says it brings high-quality DSLR effects to a smartphone.

A dual camera, though, can do a lot more, says the company, which is why HTC also has an open SDK for it. The company is confident that the new feature can lead to a lot of innovation. The 'shoot first and change focus later' as well as the copy/paste features were showcased by Siddiqui himself at the launch event. So having the open SDK for the dual camera brings developers into the fray, which Siddiqui said should bring about some exciting new apps for the device.

As before, the SDK is available on HTC's developer website and comes with distributable libraries and JavaDoc API documentation. The SDK contains two APIs—DualLens and DimensionPlus. While the former is exclusive to the HTC One (M8), the latter can run on other devices.

Other initiatives

Country head (India), Faisal Siddiqui, confirmed that the Taiwanese giant has been planning to host events for Indian developers soon, though he did not specify when exactly these would be scheduled.

The company already has developer initiatives in the United States. In addition, it is also a sponsor for the AnDevCon conference, which is the biggest Android developers' conference in the world. In 2014, the conference is scheduled from May 27 to May 30, in Boston.

No plans for an app store

In spite of all its open source efforts, HTC doesn't yet have an app store of its own. According to Siddiqui, the apps that developers come up with will currently be featured on the Google Play store only. The company currently doesn't have any plans to come up with an app store of its own. Siddiqui says that using Google Play is better, as it makes it easier for developers to create their apps and make them public.

Taking India seriously

The company reiterated its commitment to India on multiple occasions at the launch event in Delhi, but as the old saying goes, actions speak louder than words. HTC is known for its high priced devices, which has sometimes put off Indian consumers. The HTC One (M8), on the other hand, even though it is a flagship model, is priced at a strategic Rs 49,900. This places the device in the high-end segment, but at a lower price than the Apple iPhone 5S and Samsung's Galaxy S5. The pricing is an indicator of how serious HTC is about the Indian market.

At the same event, HTC launched its Desire 210 smartphone, which is a budget model aimed at a lower market segment. Interestingly, this was also the global launch for the device. A global launch is something that is not usually seen in India, considering the Indian market's uniqueness and price sensitivity.

The launch of the M8 and Desire 210 was also accompanied by the launch of the Desire 816 smartphone, which is a mid-range device priced in the Rs 24,000 bracket. So, the company launched three devices, one each in the budget, mid-range and high-end segments, further demonstrating that India is a market that HTC means to take seriously.

The flagship device, though, is the one being talked about the most, all over the world. The HTC M8 has a 90

> "The Sense UI indeed offers a lot of scope to developers. The Blinkfeed, which is one of its primary components, can easily be a developer's dream. For the uninitiated, the Blinkfeed is a compilation of your entire social network, news and some other apps"

per cent metal body along with a 4 Ultrapixel dual camera and a 12.7-cm (5-inch) 1080x1920 pixel screen. The device runs the Android 4.4 KitKat operating system and is powered by the 2.5 GHz Qualcomm Snapdragon 801 quad core processor.

The new device has quite a legacy to live up to, and HTC seems to have kept up its pace of innovation. Its predecessor, the HTC One, took more than its share of awards and was recently ranked the best smartphone at the MWC 2014. The M8 has already been shortlisted to be among the best smartphones in the world, by multiple national and international sources. And with the new open source initiatives, it seems well on its way to proving people's predictions right. END

Learn the Concept of Set Theory with Maxima

We have been experimenting with Maxima, a powerful Computer Algebraic System (CAS) for quite a while now in this series of articles. Maxima is a free and open source project that is continually being developed and improved upon. It evolved from Macsyma, which is now almost defunct. This is the 18th article in this series and it touches upon the fundamentals of set theory, through Maxima.

Most of you have definitely heard about set theory and may already know quite a bit about sets. Let us then go about getting the maths done by the computer. In this series, we have mostly been picking up mathematical concepts we're familiar with and then figuring out how we can work with these on the computer, with very little or no programming knowledge. The same holds true for sets. Let's get started with the fundamentals, starting with how they are created.

The creation of sets

A set is an unordered collection of distinct items—any item, in any order, but unique. An item is commonly referred to as an element. If an item is contained in a set, it is commonly referred to as a member of the set. A set is typically represented by its members enclosed in braces {} and separated by commas. {6, -5, 9, 0}, {dog, cat, donkey, cow, buffalo}, {Kiran, Kasturi, Karan}, and {6, horse, sapphire} are some examples. Notice that the first three sets have related items in them, but the last one doesn't. That's perfectly fine. However, if the items in a set have relation(s) or condition(s), the set can also be expressed with that relation(s) or condition(s) mentioned within braces {}. For example, {All human beings younger than 35 years}, {All positive even numbers, All multiples of 3}. In Maxima, we can straight away represent the sets in the first notation, as follows:

```
$ maxima -q
(%i1) {6, -5, 9, 0};
(%o1)                    {- 5, 0, 6, 9}
```

```
(%i2) {dog, cat, donkey, cow, buffalo};
(%o2)                    {buffalo, cat, cow, dog, donkey}
(%i3) {Kiran, Kasturi, Karan};
(%o3)                    {Karan, Kasturi, Kiran}
(%i4) {6, horse, sapphire};
(%o4)                    {6, horse, sapphire}
(%i5) {axe, knife, spear, axe, scissor};
(%o5)                    {axe, knife, scissor, spear}
(%i6) quit();
```

Note that as the order of items in the set doesn't matter, Maxima internally keeps them sorted, and hence displayed accordingly, as in the above examples. Also, note the last example—the duplicates are treated as a single item.

Sets can also be created from ordered lists using *setify*. Members of sets could be expressions, but may not be automatically simplified. Check out the following:

```
$ maxima -q
(%i1) setify([x, y, z]);
(%o1)                    {x, y, z}
(%i2) [x, y, z, x]; /* Ordered list */
(%o2)                    [x, y, z, x]
(%i3) setify([x, y, z, x]);
(%o3)                    {x, y, z}
(%i4) string({x^2 - 1, (x + 1) * (x -1)});
(%o4)                    {(x-1)*(x+1),x^2-1}
```

string() has been used in %i4, to just have the output on a single line. But the important thing to note is that though the two items of the list are mathematically identical, they have been preserved as two distinct items and thus do not form a set in the real sense. Such cases can be actually formed into a set by simplifying the individual items of the set using a corresponding simplification function, e.g., *rat()* for rational expressions. And operating any function on every item of a set can be achieved using *map()*. Here's an example to *get all those straight*, continuing from the above:

```
(%i5) string(map(rat, {x^2 - 1, (x + 1) * (x -1)}));
(%o5)                    {x^2-1}
(%i6) string(rat((x + 1) * (x -1)));
(%o6)                    x^2-1
(%i7) quit();
```

%i6 and %o6 shown above are just to demonstrate how *rat()* works. I know you are still wondering what this weird *map()* is and how it works. So, here are a few more examples:

```
$ maxima -q
(%i1) trigreduce(2 * sin(x) * cos(x));
(%o1)                    sin(2 x)
(%i2) {sin(2 * x), 2 * sin(x) * cos(x)};  /* Identical items */
(%o2)                    {2 cos(x) sin(x), sin(2 x)}
```

```
(%i3) map(trigreduce, {sin(2 * x), 2 * sin(x) * cos(x)});
(%o3)                    {sin(2 x)}
(%i4) string({apple / fruit + mango / fruit, (apple + mango)
/ fruit});
(%o4)           {(mango+apple)/fruit, mango/fruit+apple/
fruit}
(%i5) string(map(rat, {apple / fruit + mango / fruit, (apple +
mango) / fruit}));
(%o5)                    {(mango+apple)/fruit}
(%i6) quit();
```

In fact, the power of *map()* lies in its ability to take a function created on-the-fly, using the *lambda* notation. Here are a few examples to demonstrate *lamda()* first, and then *map()* using *lambda()*:

```
$ maxima -q
(%i1) f: lambda([x], x^3)$
(%i2) f(5);
(%o2)                    125
(%i3) lambda([x], x^3)(5);
(%o3)                    125
(%i4) lambda([x, y], x+y)(4, 6);
(%o4)                    10
(%i5) map(f, {0, 1, 2, 3});
(%o5)                    {0, 1, 8, 27}
(%i6) map(lambda([x], x^3), {0, 1, 2, 3});
(%o6)                    {0, 1, 8, 27}
(%i7) map(lambda([x, y], x+y), {a}, {3});
(%o7)
                         {a + 3}
(%i8) map(lambda([x], x^4), {-2, -1, 0, 1, 2});
(%o8)                    {0, 1, 16}
(%i9) map(g, {-2, -1, 0, 1, 2});
(%o9)           {g(- 2), g(- 1), g(0), g(1), g(2)}
(%i10) quit();
```

lambda() takes two arguments. First, a list of arguments of the function being defined, and second, the expression for the return value of the function using those arguments. %i1 defines a function 'f' with one argument, returning its cube. %i2 calls *f()*. However, the whole point of using *lambda* is to use it without defining an explicit function like *f()*. So, %i3 and %i4 demonstrate exactly that. %i6, %i7 and %i8 show how to use *lambda()* with *map()*. Note the elimination of duplicates in %o8. %i9 is another example of *map()*.

Basic set operations

Now, that's enough about the creation of different varieties of sets. Let's do some set operations. For starters, the union of sets is defined as a set with the items of all the sets, the intersection of sets is defined as a set with items common to all the sets, and the difference of two sets is defined as a set with items from the first set, but not in the second set. And here is a demonstration of these concepts:

```
$ maxima -q
(%i1) union({1, 2}, {1, 3, 4}, {1, 2, 6, 7});
(%o1)                        {1, 2, 3, 4, 6, 7}
%i2) intersection({1, 2}, {1, 3, 4}, {1, 2, 6, 7});
(%o2)                              {1}
(%i3) setdifference({1, 2}, {1, 3, 4});
(%o3)                              {2}
(%i4) quit();
```

Other basic set operations provided by Maxima are:
- *cardinality()* - returns the number of distinct items in a set
- *elementp()* - checks for an item to be a member of a set
- *emptyp()* - checks for the emptiness of a set
- *setequalp()* - compares two sets for equality
- *disjointp()* - checks for no common items in two sets
- *subsetp()* - checks for the first set to be a subset of the second set

The following walk-through demonstrates all of these operations:

```
$ maxima -q
(%i1) S1: {}$
(%i2) S2: {1, 2, 3}$
(%i3) S3: {3, 1, 5-3}$ /* Same as S2 */
(%i4) S4: {a, b, c}$
(%i5) S5: {2, 1, 2}$
(%i6) cardinality(S1);
(%o6)                              0
(%i7) cardinality(S2);
(%o7)                              3
(%i8) cardinality(S3);
(%o8)                              3
(%i9) cardinality(S4);
(%o9)                              3
(%i10) cardinality(S5);
(%o10)                             2
(%i11) elementp(b, S3);
(%o11)                           false
(%i12) elementp(b, S4);
(%o12)                           true
(%i13) emptyp(S1);
(%o13)                           true
(%i14) emptyp(S2);
(%o14)                           false
(%i15) setequalp(S1, S2);
(%o15)                           false
(%i16) setequalp(S2, S3);
(%o16)                           true
(%i17) disjointp(S1, S2);
(%o17)                           true
(%i18) disjointp(S2, S3);
(%o18)                           false
```

```
(%i19) disjointp(S3, S4);
(%o19)                           true
(%i20) disjointp(S3, S5);
(%o20)                           false
(%i21) subsetp(S1, S2);
(%o21)                           true
(%i22) subsetp(S2, S3);
(%o22)                           true
(%i23) subsetp(S3, S2);
(%o23)                           true
(%i24) subsetp(S3, S4);
(%o24)                           false
(%i25) subsetp(S5, S3);
(%o25)                           true
(%i26) subsetp(S3, S5);
(%o26)                           false
(%i27) quit();
```

Playing with set elements

After clearing the fundamentals, mostly through numerical examples, it is now time to have some fun with symbol substitution of Maxima. So let's play around some more:

```
$ maxima -q
(%i1) S: {a, b, c, a};
(%o1)                        {a, b, c}
(%i2) S: {a+b, b+c, c+d, d+a};
(%o2)              {b + a, c + b, d + a, d + c}
(%i3) subst(a=c, S);
(%o3)                      {c + b, d + c}
(%i4) subst([a=c, b=d], S);
(%o4)                        {d + c}
(%i5) subst([a=c, b=d, c=-d], S);
(%o5)                         {0}
(%i6) subst([a=1, b=2, c=-3], S);
(%o6)                  {- 1, 3, d - 3, d + 1}
(%i7) T: {S, {S}};
(%o7)  {{b + a, c + b, d + a, d + c}, {{b + a, c + b, d + a, d + c}}}
(%i8) subst([a=c, b=d, c=-d], T);
(%o8)                     {{0}, {{0}}}
(%i9) subst([a=1, b=2, c=-3], T);
(%o9)      {{- 1, 3, d - 3, d + 1}, {{- 1, 3, d - 3, d + 1}}}
(%i10) quit();
```

By: Anil Kumar Pugalia

The author is a hobbyist in open source hardware and software, with a passion for mathematics. A gold medallist from NIT Warangal and IISc Bangalore, mathematics and knowledge-sharing are two of his many passions. Apart from that, he shares his experiments with Linux and embedded systems through his weekend workshops. Learn more about him and his experiments at *http://sysplay.in*. He can be reached at *email@ sarika-pugs.com*.

"We don't look for just the skills but for a cultural fit as well"

If you are looking to future-proof your career as a developer, open source technology is clearly the way to go. The world of Big Data analytics is waiting for you with open arms. Dunnhumby, a retail analytics multinational firm, is here in India to tap the country's vast talent pool. *Diksha P Gupta* from *Open Source For You* spoke to *Yael Cosset, chief information officer, Dunnhumby*, on what the company looks for while hiring in India. Excerpts:

Q Dunnhumby hosted its first hackathon in India recently. Why was this organised?

The worst thing that can happen to any company like ours is to become complacent—to convince itself that it knows how to do something better than anybody else and never challenge its own thinking. These events are an opportunity for us and for the people involved. One objective is to give people the opportunity to face a real life challenge with real life data, while interacting with experts to think about how they would push themselves forward. The second point is that for us it is an opportunity to think about a different approach to a challenge that we give. Some of the challenges that we pose to the groups participating in hackathons are around data processing, data encryption, data modelling, and we have an answer to every single problem we have posed. But we would love to be challenged by some of the thinking that happens in such events. The results that the teams participating in hackathons produce are not as important as their approach to the problem. Organising hackathons has always resulted in some really innovative thinking. Though this one was our first in India, we have had several such hackathons in other parts of the world.

Q How is an Indian hackathon different from those happening in other geographies, and how is the talent you see in this country different from that available worldwide?

I will not say that it is better or worse, but it sure is different. The variety of people that participated in our hackathon and the mix of talent that we got was very interesting. About one-third of the participants were university graduates and the rest were professionals. However, in some markets, including the US, we see a lot more students turning up for such hackathons. In Europe, it is a bit more balanced, whereas in India, we are seeing a higher number of professionals participating. One thing that impresses me in India is that there is a common passion for data and big intellectual challenges. People are always excited to be challenged and to compete to demonstrate that they have a better edge. That is very refreshing to see, and that is why we want to keep engaging the talent here at such hackathons.

Q Big Data is an emerging concept. People talk about it, but are the companies really accepting Big Data analytics as a part of their businesses?

I am not sure of this with respect to the Indian market, but we

Yael Cosset, chief information officer, Dunnhumby

would always want more and more companies to be making better use of Big Data. The part that is important for us is that there is fantastic talent here, along with technology access, and the cultural passion for big complex challenges is more in India than in many other geographies.

Coming to your question on whether the companies are accepting Big Data, I would say that a lot of firms are realising the opportunity and have started to make use of data. For instance, in the retail industry, some companies have started making good use of Big Data analytics, but the nature of the retail industry is such that it is a new opportunity—one that is slowly evolving and is becoming bigger for the businesses here in India.

Q Do you use open source technology at Dunhummby?

Yes, a lot! We use a lot of open source technology, but we do not make our products open source. In fact, the world of big data is being majorly driven by open source technologies. We hire open source professionals as well.

Q Dunnhumby has been in India for about five years now. How much of change have you seen in Big Data analytics in the country, since you came into the business?

Dunnhumby has been into Big Data analytics for over 20 years now. Ever since we ventured into the Indian market, we have seen more and more talented individuals entering the field, who deliver better and better solutions. The other reality, which may be just specific to Dunnhumby in India, is that we have found a big way of leveraging the scale and the talent that we have in India to impact our businesses in every single market and geography in the world. We have not looked at India as a way to automate or focus on some pre-defined processes. We have always looked at the Indian team to help us support every single business we have across the globe. To do so, we have created a really tight connection between our India team here and our clients worldwide. We are exposing the teams to the entire portfolio of solutions that we give to the customers. So our team in India is the biggest, and has some of the best experts in the business and in everything we do. For us, the biggest evolution in the past five years has been that we really found the unique way to leverage our team in India to deliver value everywhere in the world, as opposed to just doing things in a limited manner.

The Indian team members do everything that we do in other offices, despite the fact that we do not have any customers here. That is the key point. We have ensured that the team here is not limited to a certain scope of work. It is important that the team looks at everything we do, so that it can help us bring it to other markets. It is clearly a great opportunity to be engaged and exposed to everything, so that you can have a clear understanding of the whole cycle. We are talking to a few potential partners right now in the Indian market. The team here is pretty instrumental in doing that.

Q What is your team size in India?

About 230 people work for us in this country.

Q Do you get the right kind of talent here or do you train them to suit your needs?

Yes, this is probably the team that has been the most successful at getting great quality talent in a timely fashion on a consistent basis. I have been very impressed by the quality of talent we have been able to acquire in India. We have acquired talent from some of the local universities as well as from the industry. It has been a very successful journey for us as far as getting the right kind of talent and business is concerned.

Q What kind of development processes do you have in India?

The developers' team in India works on data. We are always looking to introduce new development opportunities in the country. We also have some corporate functions, where we look for opportunities and leverage some of the talent available here. In a global business like ours, we need to find ways of providing the best services we can to every client we engage with. And for that you need great talent and great skills. Because of the unique position of our Indian team and our initial approach to it, the talent here is best qualified to do that work and deliver innovation and constant reinvention, whether it is on the technology front or on the corporate front.

India is a fantastic market to engage with.

Q Do you want to expand your footprint to the other parts of the country as well?

When we initially established ourselves, Gurgaon was an apt location because the IT industry was growing here. So, we were naturally attracted to the place and were able to get the desired talent. People are even ready to migrate from places like Bengaluru, Hyderabad, et al. We may think of expanding to other cities if we have some partnerships. We get a lot of talent from Bengaluru, so that is the second city that naturally comes to our mind for expansion. But all that happens only when we have some definite partnerships in the country. In fact, we have recently expanded our Gurgaon office and have taken another floor.

Q So with this new floor, do you plan to hire new talent?

Yes. The whole intention of having a new floor in the building was to get more talent as we felt the need for it. We have had a very successful year as a team. So, we are looking at opportunities coming in for the Indian team and hence the expansion. We estimate that we will reach the 300 mark in terms of manpower by next year by hiring about 65 people this year. We are not worried about hiring great talent in India. We get plenty of it.

Q You hire a lot of freshers, I understand?

Actually, it is a mix of fresh and lateral hiring. We do concentrate on a lot of fresh hiring. On an average, we have 10-12 graduates who join us. Globally, Dunhummby believes in getting the fresh graduates in. It's a model that works very well for us. We also look for interns for shorter time periods, to see if they have future potential. We hire differently compared to the other firms. We don't look for just the skills but for a cultural fit as well.

Q So what are the attributes a person must bring to the table in order to be hired at Dunhummby?

We have some core values that we want in our employees, which become a very integral part of the DNA of the people working at Dunhummby. Employees should have passion, an ability for collaboration, curiosity and courage. There has to be a mutual understanding on both sides regarding what the company is about and what the core ethics of its value systems are.

Q Do you think certifications add to one's profile when it comes to hiring at a place like Dunhummby?

Certifications do add, but they can't be the basis of hiring. If we have a candidate who is certified in the technologies that we use, it is an added advantage. But, along with it, the candidate must have the other attributes as well. **END**

A List Of
Unified Threat
Management (UTM) Appliances Vendors

Check Point Software | **Bengaluru**

Check Point UTM offers the perfect combination of proven security, easy deployment and effective management by consolidating key security applications (a firewall, VPN, intrusion prevention, antivirus and more) into a single, efficiently managed solution trusted by Fortune 100 companies. With Check Point, you can rest easy knowing your organisation is protected at the lowest possible cost of ownership. These UTM appliances deliver all-inclusive business network security.

Cisco Systems | **Bengaluru**

Cisco stands apart from the competition in the small business networking market as the only vendor that can provide a complete networking solution, which includes switching, routing, unified communications, wireless and security — all of which can be configured and managed through a single interface. Cisco SA500 Series Security Appliances, part of the Cisco Small Business Series, are all-in-one UTM solutions for small businesses. Combining a firewall, VPN, and optional IPS as well as email and content security capabilities, the Cisco SA500 Series gives small businesses the confidence of knowing that they are protected.

Cyberoam Technologies | **Ahmedabad**

Cyberoam Technologies, a Sophos Company, is a global network security appliances provider, offering future-ready security solutions to physical and virtual networks in organisations with its Next-Generation Firewalls (NGFWs) and UTM appliances. Cyberoam offers fast UTM appliances for SOHOs, SMBs and branch offices with comprehensive network security. The Cyberoam NG series offers future-ready security through its enterprise-grade security features, Gigabit ports and best-in-class hardware and software. Multiple security features integrated over a single, Layer 8 identity-based platform make security simple, yet highly effective. Cyberoam architecture supports a large number of concurrent sessions, offering high performance and throughput values compared to ASIC-based UTMs.

Special mention: The company is a pioneer and leader in identity-based UTMs:
- Its security solution authenticates a user by user name, MAC Id, IP address and session Id for strong protection against user-targeted attacks.
- Cyberoam architecture supports a large number of concurrent sessions, offering high performance and throughput values, as compared to ASIC-based UTMs.
- Extensible security architecture offers future-ready security by supporting feature enhancements that can be rapidly developed and deployed with minimum effort.
- On-appliance reporting at no additional expense offers real-time identity-based reports that quickly summarise the security scenario, allow proactive security or immediate remediation of breach, and support compliance management.
- On-appliance Web application firewall protects Web applications from hackers.
- Cyberoam is among the few UTMs to have an IPv6 Gold logo from the IPv6 Forum.

D-Link | **Mumbai**

D-Link UTM firewalls provide comprehensive security services, such as NetDefend IPS, antivirus and Web content filtering. D-Link's NetDefend firewalls, in conjunction with D-Link managed switches, enhance business networks through a unique combination of D-Link technology called ZoneDefense, a proactive system that guards your network against internal security risks.

Dell SonicWALL | Bengaluru

As a multi-service platform, Dell SonicWALL's line of network security appliances incorporates the broadest level of protection available through Unified Threat Management (UTM). UTM combines multiple security features into a single platform to protect against attacks, viruses, Trojans, spyware and other malicious threats. Complexity is reduced and management is simplified because multiple layers of protection are delivered under this single management console.

Fortinet | Bengaluru

Fortinet's UTM security platform, FortiGate, provides you with the ability to protect your network with the fastest firewall technology in the market. Users also have the freedom to deploy the wide range of security technologies available to fit their dynamic network environment. FortiGate network security solutions include the broadest range of technologies in the industry to give users the flexibility they need to protect their dynamic network.

Juniper Networks | Bengaluru

Juniper Networks Unified Threat Management provides a solution to the most challenging security problems. It is available with Juniper Networks SRX Series Services gateways, the only carrier-class security solution consolidating UTM content security services with routing and switching in a single, high-performance and cost-effective network device. This consolidation enables organisations to securely, reliably and economically deliver powerful new services and applications to all locations and users with superior service quality.

McAfee Software | Bengaluru

With the increased number of network-based applications and the exponential growth of threats, traditional firewalls are inadequate when it comes to protecting network data. McAfee Firewall Enterprise is a next-generation firewall that restores control and protection to an organisation's network. With it, firms can discover, control, visualise and protect their users, network applications and infrastructure.

McAfee Firewall Enterprise offers unprecedented levels of application control and threat protection. Advanced capabilities, such as application visualisation, reputation-based global intelligence, automated threat feeds, encrypted traffic inspection, intrusion prevention, anti-virus and content filtering, block attacks before they occur.

Trustwave | Mumbai

Trustwave UTM provides a comprehensive set of integrated network security technologies designed to defend against external threats, while also offering protective measures from within the network. UTM also provides rogue device detection and internal vulnerability scanning, on a single appliance, both of which are delivered by Trustwave as a fully managed service. Trustwave UTM services reduce the burden of network security management, eliminate fragmented network security controls, and conform to compliance and audit requirements.

WatchGuard Technologies | Bengaluru

WatchGuard UTM solutions provide complete security for fully integrated, multifaceted protection from network threats. WatchGuard appliances combine with powerful security subscriptions to offer comprehensive protection from malware. All security capabilities are managed from one intuitive console, with centralised logging and reporting features for an up-to-the-minute view of network security activity. As the threat landscape is always changing, WatchGuard solutions are designed to be able to easily add new network defence capabilities through security subscriptions, so that costly hardware upgrades are not necessary.

LINUX PRINCIPLE ENGINEER

Company: Altimetrik India
Exp: 8-13
Location: Bengaluru/Bangalore
Job Id: 060314002604

LINUX ADMINISTRATOR

Company: Yash Technologies Pvt ltd
Exp: 10-15
Location: Hyderabad / Secunderabad
Job Id: 200314003252

SAP HANA DBA WITH SUSE LINUX

Company: Synophic Systems INC
Exp: 6-11
Location: Bengaluru/Bangalore
Job Id: 180314003023

LINUX WLAN DEV ENGINEER

Company: Calsoft Labs India Pvt. Ltd.
Exp: 5-10
Location: Chennai
Job Id: 260414900491

LINUX ADMINISTRATOR - ENGINEERING

Company: Dfuse Technologies Ltd
Exp: 5-10
Location: Hyderabad / Secunderabad
Job Id: 220414003804

LINUX DEVICE DRIVER ENGINEER

Company: Mindlance India Pvt. Ltd.
Exp: 6-10
Location: Chennai
Job Id: 100414002192

SOFTWARE ENGINEER - LINUX

Company: Symantec Software India Pvt Ltd
Exp: 9-12
Location: Pune
Job Id: 260414002797

SR. LINUX ADMINISTRATOR

Company: Zensar Technologies
Exp: 8-11
Location: Hyderabad / Secunderabad
Job Id: 170414004481

LINUX DEVICE DEVELOPER

Company: Smartplay Technologies (I) Pvt.
Ltd
Exp: 7-10
Location: Bengaluru/Bangalore
Job Id: 040414002612

LINUX ADMINISTRATOR

Company: Transs Global Solutions
Exp: 8-10
Location: Hyderabad / Secunderabad
Job Id: 260414001382

SR. SYSTEM ADMINISTRATOR (LINUX)

Company: EMC Data Storage Systems
(India) Pvt. Ltd.
Exp: 9-12
Location: Bengaluru/Bangalore
Job Id: 150414004881

LEAD SOFTWARE ENGINEER - LINUX

Company: Great Software Laboratory Pvt.
Ltd.
Exp: 5-10
Location: Pune
Job Id: 030414900793

DEPLOYMENT LEAD (LINUX/UNIX)

Company: IGT Solutions Pvt. Ltd.
Exp: 6-10
Location: Gurgaon
Job Id: 250414003876

LINUX SYSTEM ADMINISTRATOR

Company: Oracle India Pvt. Ltd.
Exp: 6-11
Location: Bengaluru/Bangalore
Job Id: 120214000132

ENGINEER - LINUX

Company: KPIT Technologies Ltd.
Exp: 7-12
Location: Pune
Job Id: 220414002294

Search man pages with these commands

Here are a few commands that can come handy while searching through man pages in Linux.

```
$man -k ssh
```

The above command will show all available commands that contain the word *ssh* in their description.

Also, if you need to check short descriptions of the command, you can use the following:

```
$whatis ssh
```

Or:

```
$man -f ssh
```

—Somnath Sarode,
somnathsarode@gmail.com

ispell: A spell check for UNIX

This is a program used to perform a very basic spell check from the command line. Here is a tip that lets you know how to use *ispell*.

First, install it if it's not already installed, by running the following command:

```
#sudo apt-get install aspell aspell-en
```

Now, to see *ispell* in action, run the command shown below:

```
#ispell <filename>
```

You now have the option of several actions that you can take on misspelled words found in the file.

Type the number 'n' to replace the misspelled word.

Type 'R' to replace the misspelled word with a word that you wish to replace it with.

Press 'A' to ignore that misspelled word in this entire *ispell* session.

Press 'Q' to quit the program.

Press the space bar to ignore that misspelled word just once.

Press 'I' to ignore all the misspelled words.

—Pankaj Rane,
pankaj.rane2k8@gmail.com

Find user accounts without passwords

Open a terminal window and enter the following command, which will display all user accounts without passwords:

```
#awk -F: '($2 == "") {print}' /etc/shadow
```

—Suresh Jagtap,
smjagtap@gmail.com

Gaining remote access using *ssh* on a specific port

To connect to a remote Linux system, we often use *ssh*, which is a program for logging into a remote machine and executing commands on it. By default, *ssh* uses Port Number 22 to communicate. Here is a tip that lets you connect to the server with *ssh* without using the default port.

```
#ssh -p port-number root@host-name
```

– Baranitharan Krishnamoorthy,
baraninandhu@gmail.com

Unmount that stubborn USB device

I often encounter a peculiar and irritating problem with pen drives and USB storage devices. I am not able to eject/unmount these devices, and get the error message: 'The device is busy.' One simple solution is to run the command *sync* to flush out incomplete buffers, and then run:

```
$sudo umount
```

There are, of course, more sophisticated methods, but try this simple solution first to resolve this irritating problem.

—Dr Parthasarathy S,
drpartha@gmail.com

Force file system check during the next reboot

Here is a method that allows you to force a Linux-based system to run the *fsck* command on the next boot of the system. *fsck* is used to check and optionally repair one or more Linux file systems.

To run this forcibly, go to the root directory and create a file named 'forcefsck' as shown below:

```
#cd /
```

```
#touch forcefsck
```

The file *forcefsck* will be deleted automatically after *fsck* is finished.

This will only run the full file system check on the next reboot of the system.

—*Munish Kumar,*
munishtotech@gmail.com

Know your CPU

Running the following command on the terminal can give you the entire details of the CPU being used in your system:

```
#lscpu
```

—*Rahul Mahale,*
rahul.mahale123@gmail.com

Access the Windows desktop

There is a powerful utility (command) on Linux to access the remote desktop of any Windows system. The *rdesktop* is found already installed in many Debian-based systems. If not, it can be installed by running the following command:

```
$sudo apt-get install rdesktop
```

It uses Remote Desktop Protocol (RDP) for remote access. In order to access any Windows desktop, go to the terminal and type the following command:

```
rdesktop ip-address -u username -p password
```

For example:

```
$rdesktop 172.16.1.1 -u ajintha -p AUrAngAbAd
```

It will log on to the Windows system in the network that has the following IP address: 172.16.1.1, with the username *ajintha* and password *AUrAngAbAd.* It will show the Windows desktop of this system. Now, you can operate this Windows system from your Linux system!

—*Tushar Kute,*
tushar@tusharkute.com

Installing *.bin* files in Linux

We often download software as an execute file with the extension *.bin* and then do not know how to install it. Here are a few steps that will let you run the *.bin* file in Linux.

First, change the file mode bits of the downloaded *.bin* file using the following command:

```
$cd /path/to/your/bin
$sudo chmod a+x <yourbinfile>.bin
```

Now run the executable by using ./

```
$./<yourbinfile>.bin
```

—*Kiran P S,*
pskirann@gmail.com

Delete specific commands from *History*

Use the 'up' arrow to browse through the history of commands that have been used in the terminal and go to the command you want to delete. For example:

```
#cat /etc/passwd
```

Now press *Ctrl+u*

This will delete the selected command for *History.*

To check if it is deleted or not, run the following command:

```
#history
```

The output of the above command will show a blank with the * symbol in place of the deleted command.

—*Naresh Kumar,*
nrshvn@gmail.com

Finding the biggest files in Linux

Here is a command that will help you find the biggest files in the current directory:

```
$ls -lSrh
```

The 'r' causes the large files to be listed at the end, and the 'h' gives human readable output.

—*Munish Kumar,*
munishtotech@gmail.com

DVD OF THE MONTH

Lightweight and easy-to-use Linux distros are the flavours of this month's DVD.

Sabayon Linux 14.05 (64-bit) GNOME:

A modern and easy-to-use Linux distribution based on Gentoo that works out-of-the-box. It comes with a wide number of applications that are ready for use. A media centre mode lets you convert your computer into an XBMC-based media centre.

Elementary OS 0.2 (64-bit):

A lightweight operating system for your desktop, this free replacement for Windows on the PC, and OS X on the Mac, comes with a fast Web browser and an app store with thousands of apps. Luna, the latest release, has been engineered from the ground up to be light on its toes. It starts up quickly, logs in instantly, and uses the bare minimum of resources so that your apps enjoy a speed boost as well.

OpenMandriva Lx 2014.0 (32-bit):

This is a full-featured Linux-based OS for the desktop and server. 'A pinch of community, a pinch of passion, a pinch of innovation, flavoured with fun'—this is how the OpenMandriva Association describes the development of OpenMandriva Lx. It comes with a powerful variant of the 3.13.11 kernel that has been configured with desktop system performance and responsiveness in mind.

wattOS R8 (32-bit):

A fast desktop Linux distribution based on Debian, it comes with a lightweight Openbox window manager as its default user interface. The Microwatt version of wattOS included in the OSFY DVD is capable of running on hardware with smaller memory footprint.